BBC
goodfood
BAKES & CAKES

10 9 8 7 6

First published in 2004 by BBC Books, an imprint of Ebury Publishing
A Random House Group Company. This revised edition published 2014.

Photographs © BBC Worldwide 2004
Recipes © BBC Worldwide 2004
Book design © Woodlands Books Ltd 2014
All the recipes contained in this book first appeared in BBC Good Food Magazine.

The Random House Group Ltd Reg. No. 954009

Addresses for companies within the Random House Group Ltd can be found at www.randomhouse.co.uk

Penguin Random House is committed to a sustainable future
for our business, our readers and our planet. This book is made
from Forest Stewardship Council® certified paper.

Edited by Cassie Best
Commissioning Editor: Lizzy Gray
Project Editor: Lizzy Gaisford
Designers: Interstate Creative Partners Ltd
Design Manager: Kathryn Gammon
Production: Alex Goddard

Printed and bound by Firmengruppe APPL, aprinta druck, Wemding, Germany
Colour origination by Dot Gradations Ltd, UK

ISBN 9781849908665

PICTURE AND RECIPE CREDITS

BBC Good Food magazine and BBC Books would like to thank the following people for providing photos. While every effort has been made to trace and acknowledge all photographers, we should like to apologize should there be any errors or omissions.

Marie-Louise Avery p31, p143, p145, p157, p195; Steve Baxter p139; Martin Brigdale p65, p119; Linda Burgess p39, p47, p67, p73, p101, p141; Jean Cazals p201; Mike English p113; Gus Filgate p211; Will Heap p45, p83, p95, p131, p183; Adrian Lawrence p75, p109, p147; David Munns p11, p19, p41, p57, p61, p69, p87, p107, p115, p129, p137, p177; Myles New p127; Lis Parsons p187; Michael Paul p27, p29, p85, p99, p105, p133, p167, p193; Craig Robertson p25, p37, p51; Howard Shooter p13; Maja Smend p171; Simon Smith p103, p209; Roger Stowell p43, p53, p55, p63, p93, p117, p125, p161, p189, p203, p205; Rob Streeter p169; Adrian Taylor/Bill Reavell/Niall McDiarmid p23; Ian Wallace p17; Philip Webb p15, p33, p35, p59, p77, p81, p89, p153, p165, p173, p179, p185, p187, p191; Simon Wheeler p21, p79, p111, p123, p135, p151, p155, p159, p183, p199, p207; Jonathan Whittaker p149; Geoff Wilkinson p49, p91, p175; Tim Young p71, p97, p121, p181, p197.

All the recipes in this book were created by the editorial team at Good Food and by regular contributors to BBC magazines.

BBC goodfood
BAKES & CAKES

Editor **Mary Cadogan**

BBC BOOKS

Contents
. . . .

Introduction

. . . .

When the stresses of everyday life start to get to me, I find a session in the kitchen doing a bit of light cake making is the perfect answer. Cake making is sheer indulgence – nobody really needs a cake – though that's part of the pleasure. And the simple actions of beating together butter and sugar, folding in flour and rubbing mixtures together are enormously therapeutic.

Add to that the delicious smells that fill the house and the delight of all who share your baked offering, and the pleasure is complete. And whatever you make, it will always be a million times better than anything you could buy.

The cakes, biscuits and bakes in this book are all essentially very simple to make whether you are a beginner or an experienced baker, and you won't need loads of special equipment. You will find every cake you would ever want to make in this revised and updated edition, from the classic recipes for shortbread and flapjacks, to exciting new ideas such as *Blueberry Cheesecake Gateau*, *Pumpkin and Ginger Teabread* and *Strawberry and Cinnamon Torte*.

So why wait? Get out your mixing bowl and spoon and get baking – you know it makes sense.

Mary Cadoga

Mary Cadogan
BBC *Good Food* Magazine

Notes &
Conversion Tables
· ·

NOTES ON THE RECIPES
- Eggs are large in the UK and Australia and extra large in America unless stated.
- Wash fresh produce before preparation.
- Recipes contain nutritional analyses for 'sugar', which means the total sugar content including all natural sugars in the ingredients, unless otherwise stated.

OVEN TEMPERATURES

GAS	°C	°C FAN	°F	OVEN TEMP.
¼	110	90	225	Very cool
½	120	100	250	Very cool
1	140	120	275	Cool or slow
2	150	130	300	Cool or slow
3	160	140	325	Warm
4	180	160	350	Moderate
5	190	170	375	Moderately hot
6	200	180	400	Fairly hot
7	220	200	425	Hot
8	230	210	450	Very hot
9	240	220	475	Very hot

APPROXIMATE WEIGHT CONVERSIONS
- All the recipes in this book list both imperial and metric measurements. Conversions are approximate and have been rounded up or down. Follow one set of measurements only; do not mix the two.
- Cup measurements, which are used in Australia and America, have not been listed here as they vary from ingredient to ingredient. Kitchen scales should be used to measure dry/solid ingredients.

Good Food is concerned about sustainable sourcing and animal welfare. Where possible, humanely reared meats, sustainably caught fish (see fishonline.org for further information from the Marine Conservation Society) and free-range chickens and eggs are used when recipes are originally tested.

SPOON MEASURES

Spoon measurements are level unless otherwise specified.

- 1 teaspoon (tsp) = 5ml
- 1 tablespoon (tbsp) = 15ml
- 1 Australian tablespoon = 20ml (cooks in Australia should
  measure 3 teaspoons where 1 tablespoon is specified in a recipe)

APPROXIMATE LIQUID CONVERSIONS

METRIC	IMPERIAL	AUS	US
50ml	2fl oz	¼ cup	¼ cup
125ml	4fl oz	½ cup	½ cup
175ml	6fl oz	¾ cup	¾ cup
225ml	8fl oz	1 cup	1 cup
300ml	10fl oz/½ pint	½ pint	1¼ cups
450ml	16fl oz	2 cups	2 cups/1 pint
600ml	20fl oz/1 pint	1 pint	2½ cups
1 litre	35fl oz/1¾ pints	1¾ pints	1 quart

Cherry & marzipan cake

A special-occasion cake from *Good Food* reader and baker Carrie Hill.

 1 hour 55 minutes   12

- 200g/8oz butter, softened, plus extra for greasing
- 200g/8oz caster sugar
- 4 eggs, beaten
- 200g/8oz self-raising flour
- 200g/8oz glacé cherries, chopped
- 100g/4oz ground almonds
- 2–3 drops almond extract
- 250g/9oz marzipan
- 50g/2oz blanched almonds, halved lengthways
- icing sugar, for dusting

1 Heat oven to 160C/140C fan/gas 3. Butter and line a deep 20cm-round cake tin. Beat the butter and sugar in a bowl until light and creamy. Pour in the eggs a little at a time and beat well after each addition. Mix in the flour one-third at a time.

2 Fold in the cherries, ground almonds and almond extract until evenly mixed. Spoon half the mixture into the tin.

3 Roll out the marzipan to a 19cm/7½in circle. Lay this on top of the cake mixture in the tin, then cover with the rest of the mixture. Level, and scatter the almonds on top.

4 Bake for 1½ hours, or until a skewer inserted into the centre comes out clean; cover with foil after 1 hour, if the cake is getting too brown. Leave to cool in the tin for 20 minutes, then turn out on to a wire rack and cool completely. Dust with icing sugar.

PER SERVING 479 kcals, protein 8g, carbs 57g, fat 26g, sat fat 10g, fibre 2g, sugar 35g, salt 0.57g

Devonshire honey cake

This cake is based on a recipe by food writer Geraldene Holt, who lived in Devon for many years.

 1½ hours   12

- 200g/8oz unsalted butter, plus extra for greasing
- 250g/9oz clear honey, plus about 2 tbsp extra to glaze
- 100g/4oz dark muscovado sugar
- 3 eggs, beaten
- 300g/10oz self-raising flour

1 Heat oven to 160C/140C fan/gas 3. Butter and line a 20cm-round loose-bottomed cake tin. Cut the butter into pieces and drop into a medium pan with the honey and sugar. Melt slowly over a low heat. When liquid, increase the heat under the pan and boil for about 1 minute. Leave to cool.

2 Beat the eggs into the cooled honey mixture using a wooden spoon. Sift the flour into a large bowl and pour in the egg-and-honey mixture, beating until it is a smooth batter.

3 Pour the mixture into the tin and bake for 50 minutes –1 hour until the cake is golden brown, well risen and springs back when pressed.

4 Turn the cake out onto a wire rack. Warm the extra 2 tablespoons of the honey in a small pan and brush over the top of the cake to glaze, then leave to cool.

PER SERVING 336 kcals, protein 4g, carbs 43g, fat 17g, sat fat 10g, fibre 1g, sugar 25g, salt 0.29g

Squidgy pear & hazelnut–chocolate spread cake

· ·

For a perfect squidgy centre this brownie-like chocolate cake should still have a little wobble when you take it out of the oven.

🕐 1 hour   🕐 8

- 50g/2oz unsalted butter, softened, plus extra for greasing
- 400g jar hazelnut chocolate spread
- 3 eggs, at room temperature
- 140g/5oz self-raising flour
- 25g/1oz cocoa powder
- 2 ripe but not squishy pears, peeled, quartered and cored (pears with a rounder shape work well)
- 2 tbsp apricot jam, warmed and passed through a sieve
- 50g/2oz whole blanched hazelnuts
- double cream, to serve

1 Heat oven to 160C/140C fan/gas 3. Butter then line a 23cm-round springform baking tin. Put the hazelnut–chocolate spread in a large bowl and add the butter, eggs and a pinch of salt. Whisk for 1 minute with electric beaters until smooth and slightly bubbly.

2 Sift in the flour and cocoa, then fold in with a spatula until smooth. Scrape into the tin and level the top. Cut four slits through the fat part of each quartered pear, then press lightly to fan out the slices. Using a pastry brush, glaze the pears with some of the apricot jam, then lift on to the cake in a clock-face pattern. Don't press the pears into the mix.

3 Scatter with the nuts and bake for 40 minutes until risen with a thin crust. The cake will have a very slight wobble when it's ready, and a skewer inserted into the middle will come out coated with soft cake batter. Brush another thin layer of the jam over the pears. Cool in the tin and serve with double cream.

· ·

PER SERVING 474 kcals, protein 9g, carbs 47g, fat 28g, sat fat 10g, fibre 5g, sugar 34g, salt 0.4g

Fruity traybake

. . . .

A moist sponge made from banana, apple, carrots and mango, topped with a fruity soft-cheese frosting.

 1 hour   15

- 175ml/6fl oz vegetable oil, plus extra for greasing
- 175g/6oz dark muscovado sugar
- 3 eggs
- 1 small ripe banana, mashed
- 140g/5oz grated eating apples
- 100g/4oz grated carrots
- 1 small mango, peeled and cut into small dice
- zest 1 lemon
- 250g/9oz self-raising flour
- 1 tsp bicarbonate of soda
- 1 tsp ground mixed spice

FOR THE ICING
- 200g/8oz icing sugar, sieved
- 75g/2½ oz passion fruit or lemon curd
- 75g/2½oz full fat soft cheese

1 Heat oven to 180C/160C fan/gas 4. Grease and line a 22cm-square tin with baking parchment. Whisk the oil and sugar in a large mixing bowl until light and fluffy. Beat in the eggs, one at a time, followed by the banana. Stir through the apples, carrots, mango and lemon zest. Combine the flour, bicarb and mixed spice in another bowl, then fold into the fruit mixture.

2 Pour the cake mixture into the tin and bake for 40 minutes, until a skewer inserted into the centre comes out clean. Cool for 10 minutes before turning out on to a wire rack.

3 To make the icing, beat together the icing sugar, passion fruit or lemon curd and the soft cheese. Spread over the top of the cake and cut it into 15 squares to serve.

. . . .
PER SERVING 339 kcals, protein 3g, carbs 45g, fat 16g, sat fat 4g, fibre 2g, sugar 33g, salt 0.4g

Authentic Yorkshire parkin

This traditional cake for Guy Fawkes' night will keep for up to 2 weeks.

 1 hour 10 minutes   16

- 200g/8oz butter, plus extra for greasing
- 1 egg
- 3 tbsp milk
- 175g/6oz golden syrup
- 100g/4oz black treacle
- 85g/3oz light muscovado sugar
- 100g/4oz medium oatmeal
- 250g/9oz plain flour
- 2 rounded tsp ground ginger
- 2 tsp bicarbonate of soda

1 Heat oven to 160C/140C fan/gas 3. Butter a deep 23cm-square cake tin and line. Beat the egg in a small bowl and stir in the milk.

2 Put the syrup, treacle, sugar and butter in a large pan and heat gently until the sugar has dissolved and the butter has melted. Remove from the heat. Mix together the oatmeal, flour, ginger and bicarbonate of soda, then stir into the syrup mixture, followed by the egg and milk. Combine well.

3 Pour the mixture into the tin and bake for 50 minutes–1 hour until the cake feels firm and a little crusty on top. Leave to cool in the tin, then turn out and peel off the paper. Wrap the parkin in clean greaseproof paper and foil and leave it for at least 3 days – this allows it to become much softer and stickier.

PER SERVING 261 kcals. protein 3g, carbs 36g, fat 13g, sat fat 8g, fibre 1g, sugar 18g, salt 0.38g

Raisin-spice cake

. . . .

You can store this cake for up to a week in a tin.

🕐 1 hour 20 minutes   🍞 10–12

FOR THE TOPPING
- 25g/1oz butter
- 25g/1oz demerara sugar
- 1 tsp ground mixed spice
- 25g/1oz chopped nuts

FOR THE CAKE
- 175ml/6fl oz unsweetened orange juice
- 175g/6oz raisins
- 175g/6oz butter
- 175g/6oz light muscovado sugar
- 250g/9oz self-raising flour
- 1 tsp ground mixed spice
- 1 tsp ground cinnamon
- 1 tsp ground ginger
- 3 eggs, beaten

1 Heat oven to 160C/140C fan/gas 3. Butter a 23cm ring tin or 20cm-round cake tin. Make the topping: chop the butter into the rest of the topping ingredients, then sprinkle into the tin.

2 Pour the juice for the cake into a large pan, then add the raisins, butter and sugar. Bring to the boil, stirring, then simmer for 5 minutes.

3 Lift off the heat; cool for 10 minutes. Sift the flour, mixed spice, cinnamon and ginger into the pan, then add the eggs and mix. Pour the mixture into the tin and smooth the top.

4 Bake for 45 minutes until firm. Cool in the tin for 5 minutes, then transfer to a wire rack to cool completely.

. . . .
PER SERVING (10) 408 kcals, protein 6g, carbs 54g, fat 20g, sat fat 11g, fibre 1g, sugar 20g, salt 0.75g

Cinnamon pineapple upside-down cake

Vanilla and cinnamon give this classic sponge a new twist. Make sure you buy a really ripe pineapple for the decorative fruit topping.

🕐 1 hour 20 minutes 🍽 8

- 200g/8oz unsalted butter, softened
- 125g/4½oz soft brown sugar
- 1 tsp ground cinnamon
- 1½ tsp vanilla bean paste
- 1 pineapple, peeled, cut into quarters, core removed, then cut into 2cm/¾in slices
- 140g/5oz golden caster sugar
- 2 eggs, plus 1 egg white, beaten
- 1½ tsp baking powder
- 200g/8oz plain flour
- 75ml/2½fl oz whole milk
- crème fraîche, to serve (optional)

1 Heat oven to 180C/160C fan/gas 4. Put 4 tablespoons of the butter into a 22cm springform cake tin and put in the oven to melt. Remove and stir in the brown sugar, cinnamon and ½ teaspoon of the vanilla paste. Arrange the pineapple in the buttery sugar mixture, tossing a little to coat. Try to fill all the gaps, so you can't see the base.

2 In a mixing bowl, beat the caster sugar and remaining butter using an electric hand whisk for 2–3 minutes until light and fluffy. Add the eggs and egg white, one at a time, and the remaining vanilla. Add the baking powder and a pinch of salt, then the flour and milk, beating until they are both incorporated. Beat for 1 minute more until smooth.

3 Spoon the batter into the tin over the pineapple slices. Bake for 1 hour, covering with foil if it starts to brown. Leave to rest for 5 minutes, then turn out on to a platter and serve warm as a pudding, with crème fraîche, if you like. Alternatively, leave to cool completely in the tin and serve as a cake.

PER SERVING 488 kcals, protein 6g, carbs 68g, fat 23g, sat fat 14g, fibre 3g, sugar 47g, salt 0.5g

Sticky ginger cake with ginger-fudge icing

You can make the cake a couple of days in advance, wrap it well, then ice it on the day of serving.

🕐 1 hour 10 minutes   🥧 16

- 200g/8oz unsalted butter, diced
- 175g/6oz molasses sugar
- 3 tbsp black treacle
- 150ml/¼ pint milk
- 2 eggs, beaten
- 4 balls stem ginger, drained from their syrup, chopped
- 300g/10oz self-raising flour
- 1 tbsp ground ginger

FOR THE ICING
- 4 tbsp ginger syrup, drained from jar
- 300g/10oz golden icing sugar, sifted
- 140g/5oz unsalted butter, softened
- 2 tsp lemon juice

1 Heat oven to 160C/140C fan/gas 3. Butter and line the base of a 23cm-round cake tin. Gently melt the butter, sugar and treacle in a large pan; cool briefly, then stir in the milk. Beat in the eggs and add the chopped stem ginger. Sift the flour, ground ginger and a pinch of salt into the warm mixture. Combine thoroughly.

2 Spoon the cake mixture into the tin and level the surface. Bake for 30–35 minutes or until firm and risen. Cool in the tin for an hour, then transfer to a wire rack.

3 Skewer the top of the cooled cake all over, then pour over 2 tablespoons of the ginger syrup for the icing. Beat together the icing sugar, butter, lemon juice and the remaining 2 tablespoons of the ginger syrup, and spread the icing over the cake.

PER SERVING 379 kcals, protein 3g, carbs 53g, fat 19g, sat fat 11g, fibre 1g, sugar 37g, salt 0.27g

Yummy-scrummy carrot cake

Light and enticingly moist, this cake keeps for up to a week in a tin.

 1¼ hours   15

- 175ml/6fl oz sunflower oil, plus extra for oiling
- 175g/6oz light muscovado sugar
- 3 eggs, lightly beaten
- 140g/5oz grated carrot (about 3 medium carrots)
- 100g/4oz raisins
- grated zest 1 large orange
- 175g/6oz self-raising flour
- 1 tsp bicarbonate of soda
- 1 tsp ground cinnamon
- ½ tsp grated nutmeg (freshly grated will give you the best flavour)

FOR THE FROSTING

- 175g/6oz icing sugar
- 1½–2 tbsp orange juice

1 Heat oven to 180C/160C fan/gas 4. Oil and line the base and sides of an 18cm-square cake tin. Tip the sugar into a large mixing bowl, pour in the oil and add the eggs. Lightly mix, then stir in the grated carrots, raisins and orange zest.

2 Mix the flour, soda and spices, then sift into the bowl. Lightly mix all the ingredients.

3 Pour the mixture into the prepared tin and bake for 40–45 minutes, until the cake feels firm and springy when you press it in the centre. Cool in the tin for 5 minutes, then turn it out, peel off the paper and cool on a wire rack.

4 Beat together the frosting ingredients in a small bowl until smooth. Set the cake on a serving plate and drizzle the icing over the top. Leave to set, then cut into squares.

PER SERVING 265 kcals, protein 3g, carbs 39g, fat 12g, sat fat 2g, fibre 1g, sugar 24g, salt 0.41g

Olive-oil cake

· ·

The flavour of the olive oil comes through along with the citrus fruits and the almonds.

🕐 1 hour 25 minutes   🥧 12

- oil, for greasing
- 1 orange
- 1 lemon
- 4 eggs
- 100g/4oz caster sugar
- 175g/6oz plain flour
- 1 tbsp baking powder
- 225ml/8fl oz extra virgin olive oil
- 100g/4oz blanched almonds, toasted and finely chopped
- icing sugar, for dusting

1 Heat oven to 180C/160C fan/gas 4. Oil and line the base of a 23cm-round loose-bottomed or springform cake tin. Put the orange and lemon in a pan and cover with water. Bring to the boil and leave to simmer for 30 minutes until very soft. Drain and cool. Cut away the skin from the white pith and whizz the skin to a puréed paste in a food processor.

2 In a large bowl, beat the eggs with the sugar for 7–8 minutes. Sift the flour, baking powder and a pinch of salt together, then fold lightly into the egg mixture along with the olive oil. Very gently fold in the almonds and puréed fruit skin, but don't overmix.

3 Pour the batter into the tin and bake for 45 minutes. Cool on a wire rack, then dust with icing sugar.

· ·

PER SERVING 333 kcals, protein 6g, carbs 25g, fat 24g, sat fat 3g, fibre 1g, sugar 11g, salt 0.45g

Pecan-ginger cake

Stays soft and moist in the middle, and the icing sets to a crisp meringue-like coating.

🕐 1 hour   🥧 10

- 200g/8oz butter, plus extra for greasing
- 200g/8oz self-raising flour
- 4 tsp ground ginger
- 1 tsp baking powder
- ½ tsp salt
- 350g/12oz golden syrup
- 100g/4oz light muscovado sugar
- 4 eggs, beaten
- 100g/4oz pecan nuts, roughly chopped
- 100g/4oz crystallized ginger, chopped

FOR THE TOPPING & DECORATION

- 175g/6oz golden granulated sugar
- 1 egg white
- pinch cream of tartar
- 85g/3oz sugar
- 100g/4oz pecan nut halves

1 Heat oven to 180C/160C fan/gas 4. Butter and line the base of two 20cm cake tins. Sift together the flour, ginger, baking powder and salt then rub in the butter until it resembles crumbs.

2 Beat in the syrup, sugar, eggs, pecans and ginger. Pour into the tins and bake for 45 minutes until firm. Cool in the tins for 10 minutes, then turn out on to a wire rack.

3 For the topping: put the golden sugar, egg white, cream of tartar and 2 tablespoons hot water in a bowl set over (not in) a pan of simmering water. Beat for 10 minutes. Layer the cakes with a little of the icing; swirl the rest over the top and sides.

4 For the decoration: heat the sugar with 4 tablespoons water until dissolved, then boil until it forms a caramel. Stir in the pecan halves, cool on an oiled baking sheet, then use to decorate.

PER SERVING 659 kcals, protein 7g, carbs 90g, fat 33g, sat fat 11g, fibre 2g, sugar 43g, salt 1.3g

Mocha fudge cake with coffee icing

· ·

It's big, it's rich, it's moist – and impossible to resist.

🕐 1 hour 5 minutes, plus 4 hours chilling   🍰 10

FOR THE ICING
- 175g/6oz dark chocolate, melted
- 50g/2oz unsalted butter, melted
- 150ml/¼ pint double-strength espresso
- 1 tsp vanilla extract
- 300g/10oz icing sugar

FOR THE CAKE
- 85g/3oz unsalted butter, plus extra for greasing
- 300g/10oz plain flour, plus extra for the tin
- 2 tsp baking powder
- 1 tsp vanilla extract
- 3 eggs, separated
- 125ml/4fl oz milk
- 4 tbsp instant coffee granules
- 280g/10oz caster sugar
- 85g/3oz dark chocolate, melted
- 125ml/4fl oz soured cream

1 Whisk together the cooled icing ingredients. Cover and chill for 3–4 hours.

2 Heat oven to 180C/160C fan/gas 4. Butter and flour two 20cm cake tins. Sift the flour and baking powder. Stir the vanilla into the egg yolks. Heat half the milk to boiling point, stir in the coffee to dissolve, then add the rest of the milk and cool.

3 Cream the butter and 200g/8oz of the caster sugar. Slowly whisk in the egg-yolk mixture, then the melted chocolate. Fold in the sifted dry ingredients, the cooled milk and the soured cream. Whisk the egg whites until stiff; whisk in the remaining sugar to form firm peaks. Fold the egg whites into the cake mixture and pour into the tins. Bake for 30 minutes until risen. Cool, split each cake in two and layer with the icing.

· ·

PER SERVING 627 kcals, protein 8g, carbs 103g, fat 23g, sat fat 13g, fibre 2g, sugar 77g, salt 0.42g

Blueberry-cheesecake gateau

This tall cake is spectacular, easy to make and keeps for up to a day in the fridge.

 1¼ hours, plus decorating   12

- 200g/8oz butter, softened, plus extra for greasing
- 250g/9oz self-raising flour
- 1 tsp baking powder
- 200g/8oz caster sugar
- 4 eggs
- 2 tsp vanilla extract
- 1 tbsp milk

FOR THE ICING & DECORATION
- 400g/14oz medium-fat soft cheese
- grated zest 2 limes and juice 1
- 100g/4oz icing sugar
- 200g/8oz blueberries

1 Heat oven to 180C/160C fan/gas 4. Butter and line the base of a deep 18cm-round cake tin.

2 Put the flour, baking powder, sugar, butter, eggs and vanilla into a large bowl, and beat with an electric mixer on a low speed until everything is mixed together. Increase the speed and whisk for 2 minutes. Stir in the milk.

3 Spoon the mixture into the tin and level the top. Bake the cake for about 50 minutes– 1 hour, until the cake springs back when lightly pressed. Cool, then split the cake into three layers.

4 For the icing: beat the cheese until soft, then beat in the lime zest and juice and the icing sugar. Sandwich the cake back together with two-thirds of the cheese mixture, and spread the rest on the top. Arrange the blueberries in tight circles around the top of the cake to decorate.

PER SERVING 380 kcals, protein 8g, carbs 43g, fat 21g, sat fat 9g, fibre 1g, sugar 27g, salt 0.69g

Fresh cherry cake with a hint of cinnamon

· ·

Make this cake the day before a picnic – it's sturdy and travels well.

🕐 1 hour 5 minutes   🍴 8

- 85g/3oz butter, melted, plus extra for greasing
- 140g/5oz self-raising flour
- ½ tsp ground cinnamon
- 50g/2oz golden caster sugar
- 1 egg
- 4 tbsp milk
- 350g/12oz juicy ripe cherries, stalks and stones removed
- icing sugar, for dusting

FOR THE TOPPING
- 25g/1oz plain flour
- ¼ tsp ground cinnamon
- 25g/1oz golden caster sugar
- 25g/1oz butter, diced and softened

1 Heat oven to 180C/160C fan/gas 4. Butter and line the base of a 20cm-round cake tin. Sift the flour, cinnamon and sugar into a bowl. Make a well and add the egg, milk and melted butter. Combine and beat to make a thick, smooth mixture. Spoon into the tin and smooth. Scatter the cherries over the mixture and gently press them in.

2 Tip all the topping ingredients into a bowl. Rub in the butter to make a crumblike mixture, then work until it comes together in pea-sized pieces. Scatter this over the cherries.

3 Bake for 30–35 minutes until a skewer pushed into the centre of the cake comes out clean. Leave in the tin until cool enough to handle, then tip on to a wire rack until it is completely cold.

· ·

PER SERVING 247 kcals, protein 3g, carbs 32g, fat 12g, sat fat 7g, fibre 1g, sugar 12g, salt 0.46g

Rhubarb & orange cake

Make the most of seasonal fruit in this rustic bake with almond topping – serve it warm from the oven, as a pudding, or cooled for afternoon tea.

 1 hour 40 minutes   8

- 400g/14oz rhubarb, thickly sliced
- 300g/10oz golden caster sugar
- 200g/8oz butter, softened, plus extra for greasing
- finely grated zest and juice 1 orange
- 200g/8oz self-raising flour
- 100g pack ground almonds
- 1 tsp baking powder
- 3 medium eggs
- small handful flaked almonds
- icing sugar, for dusting

1 Heat oven to 180C/160C fan/gas 4. Tip the rhubarb into a bowl and sprinkle over 50g/2oz of the sugar. Stir so the rhubarb is covered, then set aside for 30 minutes to draw out some of the juices. Meanwhile, grease and line the base and sides of a 23cm-round loose-bottomed cake tin with baking parchment.

2 Tip the remaining sugar, the butter, orange zest and juice into a large bowl, and beat with an electric whisk until well blended. Add the flour, almonds, baking powder and eggs, then beat again until smooth. Fold in the rhubarb and any juices. Spoon into the tin and level the top.

3 Sprinkle with the flaked almonds, then bake in the centre of the oven for 1 hour–1¼ hours until risen, golden and a skewer inserted into the centre comes out clean. Cover with foil if the cake starts to brown too much during cooking. Leave in the tin for 15 minutes before removing and cooling completely on a wire rack. Dust with icing sugar before serving.

PER SERVING 445 kcals, protein 6g, carbs 46g, fat 26g, sat fat 13g, fibre 2g, sugar 31g, salt 0.7g

St Lucia banana cake

This cake conjures up the taste of the Caribbean.

 1 hour 5 minutes   12

- butter, for greasing
- 350g/12oz self-raising flour
- 1 tsp bicarbonate of soda
- 2 tsp ground mixed spice
- 175g/6oz light muscovado sugar
- 4 eggs
- 200ml/7fl oz sunflower oil
- 2 bananas, mashed
- 100g/4oz pineapple, very finely chopped
- finely grated rind and juice 1 orange
- 100g pack walnuts, roughly chopped

FOR THE FROSTING & DECORATION
- 2 x 200g packs medium-fat soft cheese, at room temperature
- 200g/8oz icing sugar
- 50g/2oz honey-coated banana chips

1 Heat oven to 180C/160C fan/gas 4. Butter and line two 20cm sandwich tins. Sift the flour into a large bowl with the soda, mixed spice and sugar.

2 Whisk the eggs and the oil until smooth. Stir the egg mixture into the flour with the bananas, pineapple, orange rind and juice and walnuts; stir well. Divide between the prepared tins. Bake for 45 minutes until risen and firm. Cool for 10 minutes, then remove from the tins, peel off the paper and leave to cool completely.

3 Beat the soft cheese for the frosting until smooth. Gradually add the icing sugar to give a smooth frosting. Spread half the frosting over one cake. Put the other cake on top. Spread over the remaining icing, swirling it with a palette knife. Sprinkle over the banana chips to decorate.

PER SERVING 545 kcals, protein 10g, carbs 64g, fat 30g, sat fat 3g, fibre 2g, sugar 32g, salt 0.66g

Flourless lemon & polenta drizzle cake

This gluten-free citrus cake has a grown-up bitter edge. Serve with creamy mascarpone and black coffee.

🕐 2 hours 20 minutes, plus cooling 🍽 8

- 140g/5oz butter, softened, plus extra for greasing
- 2 lemons
- 3 eggs
- 250g/9oz golden caster sugar
- 200g/8oz ground almonds
- 175g/6oz polenta or fine cornmeal
- 1 tsp gluten-free baking powder
- mascarpone, to serve

FOR THE DRIZZLE

- 140g/5oz golden caster sugar
- juice 1 lemon

1 Grease a 23cm-round cake tin and heat oven to 180C/160C fan/gas 4. Put the lemons in a pan and cover with cold water. Bring to the boil, drain, pour over more cold water, then simmer for 1 hour until the lemons are really soft, topping up with more water, if you need to. Drain the lemons well. When cool, halve them, remove the pips and blitz in a food processor to a purée.

2 Add all the other cake ingredients and carry on blitzing until you have a loose batter. Scrape the batter into the cake tin and bake for 40–50 minutes until golden and starting to shrink away from the sides.

3 While the cake bakes, make the drizzle by mixing the sugar with the lemon juice. When the cake is ready, remove from the oven and leave to cool a little. While still warm, pour over the drizzle and leave to cool completely. Serve with mascarpone.

PER SERVING 590 kcals, protein 10g, carbs 69g, fat 31g, sat fat 11g, fibre 2g, sugar 51g, salt 0.6g

Crumbly cherry almond cake

This crumbly cake is a terrific way to enjoy fresh cherries.

🕐 1½ hours   🍽 8

- 140g/5oz butter, cut into small pieces and softened, plus extra for greasing
- 140g/5oz whole blanched almonds
- 250g/9oz self-raising flour
- 75g/2½oz ground almonds
- 140g/5oz caster sugar
- 2 eggs, beaten
- 125ml/4fl oz milk
- 300g/10oz fresh cherries, stoned and patted dry
- 25g/1oz flaked almonds

1 Heat oven to 180C/160C fan/gas 4. Butter and line the base of a 20cm-round deep cake tin. Put the blanched almonds in a small pan and heat gently, shaking occasionally, until golden brown (about 10 minutes). Cool, then whizz in a food processor until finely ground.

2 Tip the flour into a bowl and stir in the ground almonds. Rub in the butter until the mixture is crumbly. Stir in the sugar, then add the eggs, milk and cherries; mix until combined, but don't overmix.

3 Spoon into the prepared tin and smooth the top, then sprinkle the flaked almonds on top. Bake for 1 hour 10 minutes until the cake is golden on top and firm to the touch. Cool in the tin for 10 minutes, then turn out on to a wire rack to cool. Eat within 3 days.

PER SERVING 474 kcals, protein 10g, carbs 48g, fat 28g, sat fat 11g, fibre 3g, sugar 18g, salt 0.69g

Apple & cinnamon cake

· ·

Serve this warm from the oven as a tasty dessert, or cold for a picnic or lunchbox treat.

🕐 1 hour   🥧 8–10

- 250g/9oz self-raising flour
- 1 tsp ground cinnamon
- 1 tsp baking powder
- 100g/4oz light muscovado sugar
- 175g/6oz sultanas or raisins
- 125ml/4fl oz sunflower oil
- 2 eggs, beaten
- 125ml/4fl oz apple juice
- 2 dessert apples (not peeled), grated
- 25g/1oz slivered or flaked almonds
- icing sugar, for dusting

1 Heat oven to 180C/160C fan/gas 4. Line a deep 23cm-round cake tin with non-stick baking paper. Sift the flour into a bowl with the cinnamon and baking powder, then stir in the sugar and sultanas or raisins. Make a well in the centre and stir in the oil, eggs, apple juice and grated apple until well mixed.

2 Pour the mixture into the tin, scatter with almonds, then bake for 40–45 minutes until firm in the centre or a skewer inserted into the middle of the cake comes out clean. Leave to cool in the tin for about 5 minutes, then turn out and cool on a wire rack. Dust with icing sugar.

· ·

PER SERVING (10) 342 kcals, protein 6g, carbs 46g, fat 16g, sat fat 2g, fibre 2g, sugar 10g, salt 0.46g

Raspberry & blueberry lime drizzle cake

Wonderfully moist and fruity, this cake is a teatime favourite.

 1 hour 25 minutes   12

- 200g/8oz butter, softened, plus extra for greasing
- 200g/8oz golden caster sugar
- 4 eggs
- 250g/9oz self-raising flour, sifted with pinch salt
- grated zest and juice 2 limes
- 25g/1oz ground almonds
- 100g/4oz each blueberries and raspberries

FOR THE SYRUP
- 8 tbsp lime juice (about 4 limes)
- grated zest 1 lime
- 140g/5oz golden caster sugar

1 Heat oven to 180C/160C fan/gas 4. Line the base and sides of a 20cm-square cake tin and butter the paper.
2 Cream the butter and sugar together in a large bowl until light. Gradually beat in the eggs, adding a little of the flour towards the end to prevent curdling. Beat in the lime zest, then fold in the rest of the flour and the almonds. Fold in about 3 tablespoons lime juice, giving a good dropping consistency. Fold in three-quarters of the blueberries and raspberries, and turn into the prepared tin. Smooth, then scatter the remaining fruit on top. Bake for about 1 hour or until firm.
3 For the syrup: gently heat the lime juice, zest and sugar in a pan, without allowing the syrup to bubble. While the cake is still hot, prick it all over with a skewer then spoon the syrup over it.

PER SERVING 370 kcals, protein 5g, carbs 49g, fat 19g, sat fat 10g, fibre 1g, sugar 32g, salt 0.61g

Almond cake with clementines

. . . .

This cake is very moist and light, and the apricots add a juicy note – a brilliant special-occasion dessert.

 1 hour 50 minutes   8

- 100g/4oz butter, softened, plus extra for greasing
- 100g/4oz ready-to-eat dried apricots
- 175ml/6fl oz clementine juice (about 6–8 clementines)
- 100g/4oz golden caster sugar
- 2 eggs
- 50g/2oz self-raising flour
- 175g/6oz ground almonds
- ½ tsp vanilla extract
- 2 tbsp flaked almonds
- icing sugar, for dusting
- clementines in syrup (from a jar) and thick cream or Greek yogurt, to serve

1 Heat oven to 180C/160C fan/gas 4. Butter and line the base of a 20cm-round cake tin. Finely chop the apricots and put in a pan with the clementine juice. Bring to the boil, then gently simmer for 5 minutes. Leave to cool.

2 Beat the butter, sugar, eggs and flour in a bowl for 2 minutes until light and fluffy, then fold in the ground almonds, vanilla and apricots along with their juices.

3 Turn the mixture into the prepared tin and smooth. Scatter the flaked almonds on top. Bake for 40–50 minutes until firm. Cool in the tin for 5 minutes, then turn out and cool on a wire rack. Dust the cake with icing sugar. Slice, and put a wedge on each plate with a clementine. Spoon the clementine syrup from the jar over the cake and fruit. Serve with the cream or yogurt.

. . . .

PER SERVING 291 kcals, protein 6g, carbs 27g, fat 19g, sat fat 8g, fibre 2g, sugar 15g, salt 0.36g

Mango, banana & coconut cake

Buy your mangoes a couple of days ahead to ensure they are fully ripe.

 55 minutes 🥧 10

- 200g/8oz butter, softened, plus extra for greasing
- 1 medium ripe mango
- 2 ripe bananas
- 1 tsp vanilla extract
- 140g/5oz light muscovado sugar
- 2 eggs, beaten
- 50g/2oz desiccated coconut
- 200g/8oz self-raising flour
- ½ tsp bicarbonate of soda
- 1 tsp ground mixed spice

FOR THE FILLING

- 200g pack full-fat soft cheese
- 2 tsp lemon juice
- 25g/1oz icing sugar, plus extra for dusting

1 Heat oven 160C/140C fan/gas 3. Butter and line the bases of two 20cm-round sandwich tins. Peel, stone and chop the mango, then purée the flesh. Mash the bananas, then mix in half the mango purée and the vanilla.

2 Beat together the butter and sugar until light and fluffy. Beat in the eggs, a little at a time, then stir in the banana mixture and the coconut. Sift in the flour, bicarbonate of soda and spice, then fold in lightly. Divide the mixture between the tins and smooth. Bake for 30–35 minutes. Cool in the tins for 5 minutes, then turn out on to a wire rack.

3 Beat together the filling ingredients, then stir in the reserved mango. Spread one cake with the filling. Put the other cake on top and dust lightly with icing sugar.

PER SERVING 468 kcals, protein 5g, carbs 42g, fat 32g, sat fat 21g, fibre 2g, sugar 17g, salt 0.83g

English rose cake

A stunning floral layer cake, flavoured with rosewater and layered up with vanilla cream, raspberry icing and crystallised petals.

 1 hour 55 minutes   15

FOR THE CAKE
- 350g/12oz butter, softened, plus extra for greasing
- 500g/1lb 2oz golden caster sugar
- 6 eggs
- 200g/7oz full-fat natural yogurt
- 500g/1lb 2oz plain flour
- 4 tsp baking powder
- 1 tsp vanilla extract
- 1 tsp rosewater

FOR THE ROSE SYRUP, ICING & CREAM
- 140g/5oz golden caster sugar
- 1-2 tsp rosewater
- 85g/3oz raspberries, plus 100g/4oz to decorate
- 250g/9oz icing sugar
- 1 tsp vanilla extract
- 300ml pot double cream
- rose petal pieces and crystallised rose petals, to decorate

1 Heat oven to 160C/140C fan/gas 3. Grease and line the base and sides of 3 x 20cm round cake tins. Beat all the cake ingredients with an electric whisk until combined then divide between the cake tins. Bake for 45 minutes. Leave in the tins for 10 minutes. Remove from the tins and transfer to a wire rack to cool.

2 To make the syrup, heat the sugar in a pan with 100ml/4fl oz water until dissolved. Bubble for 1–2 minutes, then remove from the heat. Add the rosewater to taste. Spoon half the syrup over the 3 sponges and set aside.

3 Add 2 tablespoons of the syrup to the raspberries and crush with a fork then push through a sieve into a bowl and discard the seeds. Sift in the icing sugar and mix to a smooth icing. In a second bowl, add the vanilla and 2 tablespoons of the syrup to the cream and whisk until it holds soft peaks. Chill.

4 Place one cake, flat-side up, and top with half the cream and a third of the remaining raspberries. Repeat then top with the last cake. Smooth the icing over the top. Decorate.

PER SERVING 665 kcals, protein 7g, carbs 84g, fat 33g, sat fat 20g, fibre 2g, sugar 58g, salt 0.7g

Citrus poppy seed cake

This treat can be stored in the fridge for up to 3 days.

 1 hour 5 minutes   10

- 175g/6oz butter, softened, plus extra for greasing
- 175g/6oz caster sugar
- 3 eggs, beaten
- 250g/9oz self-raising flour
- 50g/2oz poppy seeds
- grated rind 2 oranges
- grated rind 2 lemons
- 4 rounded tbsp natural yogurt

FOR THE TOPPING & DECORATION
- 250g tub mascarpone
- grated rind and juice 1 small orange
- 3 tbsp orange or lemon curd
- grated rind 1 lemon

1 Heat oven to 150C/130C fan/gas 2. Butter and line the base of a deep 20cm-round cake tin. Using a wooden spoon, beat together the butter, sugar, eggs, flour, poppy seeds, citrus rinds and yogurt until smooth.

2 Spread the mixture in the tin and bake for 45–50 minutes until just firm. Cool in the tin for 10 minutes, then turn out and cool on a wire rack. Peel off the paper.

3 Meanwhile, mix the mascarpone for the topping with enough orange juice to make a spreadable icing. Lightly swirl in the curd to give a marbled effect. Roughly spread over the top and sides of the cake, and scatter the grated citrus rind over the top to decorate.

PER SERVING 483 kcals, protein 7g, carbs 48g, fat 31g, sat fat 11g, fibre 2g, sugar 18g, salt 0.74g

Apple cake in a nutshell

An all-in-one cake, topped with fresh apples, then glazed for a beautiful finish.

 1¼ hours   12

- 175g/6oz butter, melted, plus extra for greasing
- 3 eggs
- 350g/12oz self-raising flour
- 2 tsp ground cinnamon
- 175g/6oz light muscovado sugar
- 3 medium eating apples, such as Cox's, unpeeled and cored
- 100g/4oz dates, stoned and cut into pieces
- 100g/4oz blanched hazelnuts, roughly chopped
- 3 tbsp apricot compote

1 Heat oven to 180C/160C fan/gas 4. Butter and line the base of a 20cm-round cake tin. Beat the eggs into the cooled butter. Put the flour, cinnamon and sugar into a separate bowl, and mix well.

2 Cut 2 of the apples into chunks. Stir the chunks into the flour with the dates and half of the hazelnuts. Mix well. Pour the egg-and-butter mixture into the flour mixture and stir gently. Spoon into the tin and smooth.

3 Cut the remaining apple into thin slices and arrange over the cake. Sprinkle the remaining hazelnuts over the apple slices. Bake for 50 minutes–1 hour, or until a skewer inserted into the centre of the cake comes out clean. Cool in the tin for 5 minutes, then turn out on a wire rack. While the cake is still warm, heat the apricot compote. Brush over the cake, then cool completely.

PER SERVING 377 kcals, protein 6g, carbs 49g, fat 19g, sat fat 8g, fibre 3g, sugar 15g, salt 0.61g

Orange & almond cake

. . . .

This unconventionally made bittersweet cake freezes beautifully.

 50 minutes   12

- 175g/6oz butter, softened, plus extra for greasing
- 1 medium orange
- 175g/6oz light muscovado sugar
- 3 eggs
- 175g/6oz self-raising flour
- ½ tsp bicarbonate of soda
- 50g/2oz ground almonds
- icing sugar, for dredging

1 Heat oven to 190C/170C fan/gas 5. Butter and line the base of a deep 23cm-round cake tin. Cut the whole orange – skin, pith, flesh, the lot – into pieces. Remove any pips, then whizz the orange pieces in a food processor to a finely chopped purée.

2 Tip the butter, sugar, eggs, flour, bicarbonate of soda and almonds into the processor, and whizz for 10 seconds, until smooth. Pour into the prepared tin and smooth the top.

3 Bake for 25–30 minutes, until the cake is risen and brown. Allow to cool in the tin for 5 minutes before turning out on to a wire rack. Dredge thickly with icing sugar before serving.

. . . .
PER SERVING 266 kcals, protein 4g, carbs 29g, fat 16g, sat fat 8g, fibre 1g, sugar 16g, salt 0.61g

Soured cream rhubarb squares

These squares are really light, and delicious hot or cold.

 1 hour 20 minutes 15

- 100g/4oz butter, softened, plus extra for greasing
- 100g/4oz golden caster sugar
- 100g/4oz mixed nuts, roughly chopped
- 1 tsp ground cinnamon
- 250g/9oz dark muscovado sugar
- 1 egg
- 200g/8oz plain flour
- 1 tsp bicarbonate of soda
- ½ tsp salt
- 2 x 142ml pots soured cream
- 300g/10oz rhubarb, cut into 1cm/½in pieces

1 Heat oven to 180C/160C fan/gas 4. Grease and line a deep 33 x 23cm baking tin with baking paper. Melt about 15g/½oz of the butter and stir into the caster sugar, nuts and cinnamon in a bowl. Set aside.

2 Beat together the rest of the butter with the muscovado sugar and egg. When smooth and creamy, stir in the flour, bicarbonate of soda, salt and the soured cream. Lastly, stir in the rhubarb.

3 Pour the rhubarb mixture into the prepared tin and sprinkle with the sugar-and-nut topping. Bake for 30–35 minutes or until a skewer inserted in the centre of the cake comes out clean. Serve immediately as a pudding, or leave to cool and cut into squares. Keeps for 4–5 days in an airtight tin.

PER SQUARE 277 kcals, protein 4g, carbs 37g, fat 13g, sat fat 7g, fibre 1g, sugar 24g, salt 0.63g

Strawberry & cinnamon torte

. . . .

The perfect crumbly dessert for a summer Sunday lunch or dinner.

🕐 1¼ hours   🥧 6–8

- 175g/6oz butter, softened, plus extra for greasing
- 175g/6oz ground almonds
- 175g/6oz golden caster sugar
- 175g/6oz self-raising flour
- 1 tsp ground cinnamon
- 1 egg, plus 1 egg yolk
- 450g/1lb strawberries, hulled and sliced
- icing sugar, for dusting
- whipped double cream mixed with Greek yogurt, to serve

1 Heat oven to 180C/160C fan/gas 4. Butter and line the base of a loose-bottomed 23cm-round cake tin. In a food processor, mix the ground almonds, butter, sugar, flour, cinnamon, egg and egg yolk until evenly mixed.

2 Tip half the mixture into the tin and smooth. Spread the strawberries on top. Top with the remaining cake mixture; spread smooth.

3 Bake for 1 hour–1 hour 5 minutes. Check after 40 minutes – if the torte is getting too brown, cover loosely with foil. When cooked, the torte should be slightly risen and dark golden brown.

4 Cool slightly, then remove from the tin. Slide on to a plate and dust with icing sugar. Serve warm, in wedges, with spoonfuls of cream and Greek yogurt.

. . . .

PER SERVING (8) 491 kcals, protein 9g, carbs 45g, fat 32g, sat fat 13g, fibre 3g, sugar 23g, salt 0.68g

Blueberry soured cream cake

Blueberries bake really well in cakes, as their purple skins keep in their juicy centres.

 1 hour 25 minutes 🕐 10

- 175g/6oz butter, softened, plus extra for greasing
- 175g/6oz golden caster sugar
- 3 eggs
- 200g/8oz self-raising flour
- 1 tsp baking powder
- 2 tsp vanilla extract
- 142ml pot soured cream
- 3 x 125g punnets blueberries

FOR THE FROSTING
- 200g tub full fat soft cheese
- 100g/4oz icing sugar

1 Heat oven to 180C/160C fan/gas 4. Butter and line the base of a 23cm-round cake tin. Put the butter, sugar, eggs, flour, baking powder and vanilla in a bowl. Beat for 2–3 minutes until pale and well mixed. Beat in 4 tablespoons of the soured cream, then stir in half the blueberries.

2 Tip the mixture into the tin and level. Bake for 50 minutes, or until it feels firm to the touch and springs back when lightly pressed. Cool for 10 minutes, then take out of the tin and peel off the paper. Leave to finish cooling.

3 Beat the soft cheese with the icing sugar and the remaining soured cream until smooth and creamy. Spread over the top of the cooled cake and scatter with the remaining blueberries. The cake will keep in the fridge for a couple of days.

PER SERVING 469 kcals, protein 6g, carbs 50g, fat 29g, sat fat 17g, fibre 1g, sugar 29g, salt 0.93g

Raspberry & almond Madeira cake

This tasty cake can be made in advance but is best eaten within 2–3 days.

🕐 1½ hours   🍴 8

- 175g/6oz butter, softened, plus extra for greasing
- 175g/6oz caster sugar
- 1 tsp vanilla extract
- 3 eggs, lightly beaten
- 50g/2oz flaked almonds
- grated zest 1 orange
- 100g/4oz plain flour, sifted
- 100g/4oz self-raising flour, sifted
- 2 tbsp milk
- 200g/8oz raspberries, fresh or frozen
- icing sugar, for dusting

1 Heat oven to 160C/140C fan/gas 3. Butter and line a deep 20cm cake tin. Cream the butter and sugar in a large bowl. Beat in the vanilla, then gradually beat in the eggs to make a batter.

2 Set aside a few almonds. Crumble the rest and stir them and the zest into the batter. Fold in the sifted flours and milk, then fold in all but eight of the raspberries.

3 Put the mixture in the tin and level, then arrange the remaining raspberries on top. Sprinkle the reserved almonds over the top, and bake for 1¼ hours. Cool in the tin for 10 minutes, then on a wire rack. Dust with icing sugar.

PER SERVING 410 kcals, protein 7g, carbs 45g, fat 24g, sat fat 12g, fibre 2g, sugar 24g, salt 0.61g

Whole orange cake

The juicy flavour of a whole orange goes into this cake.

 1¾ hours   8–10

- 1 small orange
- 50g/2oz butter, melted, plus extra for greasing
- 140g/5oz caster sugar
- 3 eggs
- 85g/3oz self-raising flour
- 100g/4oz ground almonds
- crème fraîche, to serve (optional)

FOR THE ICING
- 85g/3oz icing sugar
- juice 1 small sweet orange (or enough to make a smooth pouring icing)

1 Put the orange in a pan and cover with cold water. Bring to the boil, cover and simmer for 1 hour. Remove the orange and cool.

2 Heat oven to 180C/160C fan/gas 4. Butter and line the base of a deep 20cm-round cake tin. Roughly chop the cooked orange, discarding the pips. Whizz in a food processor until smooth. Whisk the sugar and eggs until light and fluffy.

3 Sift the flour and ground almonds on to the egg mixture. Using a large metal spoon, fold gently, then add the orange purée and melted butter. Fold in gently until just mixed. Pour the cake mixture into the prepared tin. Bake for 40–45 minutes until the cake is brown and springs back when lightly pressed. Cool in the tin for 5 minutes. Mix the icing sugar and juice together, drizzle over the cake and serve with crème fraîche.

Squidgy chocolate and pomegranate torte

This rich dark chocolate sponge makes a great alternative Christmas cake, or dinner party dessert

 55 minutes 12

- 225g/8oz unsalted butter, plus extra for greasing
- 250g/9oz dark chocolate (70% cocoa), broken into squares
- 5 eggs
- 225g/8oz light muscovado sugar, squished through your fingers to remove any lumps
- 85g/3oz ground almonds
- 50g/2oz plain flour, plus an extra 1 tbsp

FOR THE TOPPING
- 150ml pot double cream, brought to the boil
- 100g bar dark chocolate (70% cocoa), roughly chopped
- 1 tbsp icing sugar, sifted
- handful pomegranate seeds

1 Grease and line a 23cm springform tin. Heat oven to 180C/160C fan/gas 4. Melt the butter and chocolate in a bowl over a pan of simmering water. Stir until smooth.

2 Whisk the eggs and sugar in a large bowl, for 5-8 minutes with electric hand beaters until thick, mousse-like and doubled in volume. Pour the chocolate mix around the edge of the bowl, then fold together using a metal spoon. Sift over the almonds, flour and ¼ tsp salt, then fold in until even. Slowly pour the batter into the tin. Bake on a middle shelf for 30-35 minutes, or until the cake is risen and set on top. Cool the cake in its tin on a rack.

3 For the topping, put the chocolate and icing sugar in a bowl, then tip the hot cream over it. Leave for 3 minutes, stir until smooth, then leave for 10 minutes. Remove the torte from its tin, then spread the icing over the top. Leave to set, then scatter with the pomegranate seeds. Serve immediately or chill for a few hours.

PER SLICE 544 kcals, protein 7g, carbs 35g, fat 40g, sat fat 22g, fibre 3g, sugar 28g, salt 0.2g

Dark chocolate & orange cake

Chocolate and orange is a classic combination.

🕐 2 hours 10 minutes, plus 1½ hours cooling 🍰 10

- butter, for greasing
- 1 Seville orange
- 3 eggs
- 300g/10oz caster sugar
- 240ml/8½fl oz sunflower oil
- 100g/4oz dark chocolate, broken into pieces and melted
- 25g/1oz cocoa powder
- 250g/9oz plain flour
- 1½ tsp baking powder

FOR THE CHOCOLATE GANACHE & DECORATION

- 200g/8oz dark chocolate, broken into pieces
- 225ml/8fl oz double cream
- candied orange zest

1 Pierce the orange with a skewer. Cook in a pan of boiling water for 30 minutes. Remove and whizz the whole orange in a food processor. Discard any pips and cool.

2 Heat oven to 180C/160C fan/gas 4. Butter and line the base of a 23cm-round cake tin. Lightly beat the eggs, sugar and oil. Gradually beat in the puréed orange and cooled, melted chocolate. Sift in the cocoa, flour and baking powder. Mix well and pour into the tin. Bake for 55 minutes–1 hour. Cool for 10 minutes, then turn out on to a wire rack.

3 Put the ganache chocolate into a heatproof bowl. Boil the cream in a pan, pour over the chocolate and stir until smooth. Cool, up to 1½ hours, until firm. Spread over the cake and decorate with the candied zest.

PER SERVING 703 kcals, protein 7g, carbs 73g, fat 45g, sat fat 16g, fibre 2g, sugar 51g, salt 0.42g

Pear, hazelnut & chocolate cake

Moist and fruity enough to serve warm with cream for pud, but just as good cold.

🕐 1½ hours 🍽 8

- 175g/6oz butter, cut into small pieces, plus extra for greasing
- 100g/4oz blanched hazelnuts
- 140g/5oz self-raising flour
- 140g/5oz golden caster sugar
- 2 eggs, beaten
- 5 small ripe Conference pears
- 50g/2oz dark chocolate, chopped into small chunks
- 2 tbsp apricot jam

1 Heat oven to 160C/140C fan/gas 3. Butter and line the base of a 20cm-round cake tin. Grind the hazelnuts in a food processor until fairly fine. Add the flour and mix briefly. Add the butter and pulse until it forms crumbs. Add the sugar and eggs, and mix briefly. Peel, core and chop 2 of the pears. Stir the pears and chocolate lightly into the cake mixture.

2 Spoon the mixture into the prepared tin and smooth the top. Peel, core and slice the remaining pears and scatter over the top of the cake. Press down lightly and bake for 50 minutes–1 hour, until firm to the touch. Cool in the tin for 10 minutes, then turn out and cool on a wire rack. Warm the jam and brush over the top. Serve warm or cold.

PER SERVING 470 kcals, protein 6g, carbs 47g, fat 30g, sat fat 14g, fibre 3g, sugar 18g, salt 0.5g

Prune & chocolate torte

Rich with brandy-steeped prunes, this is a cake for real lovers of chocolate.

 1 hour 5 minutes, plus 30 minutes soaking   8

- 250g/9oz no-soak prunes, halved
- 4 tbsp brandy
- 50g/2oz butter, plus extra for greasing
- 25g/1oz cocoa powder
- 100g/4oz dark chocolate (at least 70% cocoa solids), broken into pieces
- 175g/6oz golden caster sugar
- 4 egg whites
- 85g/3oz plain flour
- 1 tsp ground cinnamon
- lightly whipped cream or crème fraîche, to serve

1 Soak the prunes in brandy for 30 minutes. Heat oven to 190C/170C fan/gas 5. Butter a 23cm-round loose-bottomed cake tin. Put the cocoa, chocolate, butter and 140g/5oz of the sugar in a pan, add 100ml/3½fl oz hot water and gently heat until smooth then leave to cool slightly.

2 Whisk the egg whites to soft peaks, then gradually whisk in the remaining sugar. Sift the flour and cinnamon over the egg whites and gently fold in with a metal spoon, until almost combined. Add the chocolate mixture to the flour and egg whites and fold in until evenly combined.

3 Pour the mixture into the tin and arrange the prunes over the top. Sprinkle over any remaining brandy. Bake for 30 minutes until just firm. Serve with cream or crème fraîche.

PER SERVING 311 kcals, protein 5g, carbs 51g, fat 10g, sat fat 6g, fibre 3g, sugar 31g, salt 0.18g

Eggless chocolate & beetroot blitz & bake cake

Healthier than your average chocolate cake, this rich and dark bake is lighter on the calories.

 1 hour 20 minutes 12

- 100ml/3½fl oz rapeseed oil, plus extra for greasing
- 175g/6oz (drained weight) vacuum-packed beetroot (not in vinegar)
- 175g/6oz dark soft brown sugar
- 200g/8oz self-raising flour
- 1 tbsp baking powder
- 50g/2oz cocoa powder
- 200g/8oz 0% fat natural yogurt
- 2 tsp vanilla extract

FOR THE ICING & DECORATION
- 100g/4oz icing sugar
- 50g/2oz dark chocolate (at least 80% cocoa solids)
- 1 tbsp cocoa powder
- 3 tbsp skimmed milk
- dark chocolate shavings (optional)

1 Heat oven to 180C/160C fan/gas 4. Grease and line a deep 20cm springform cake tin with baking parchment. Tip the beetroot into a food processor and whizz to a purée. Add the remaining cake ingredients, along with ¼ teaspoon salt, and blend until well combined. Scrape into the tin, level the surface and bake for 50 minutes–1 hour or until a skewer inserted into the centre of the cake comes out clean.

2 Leave the cake to cool in the tin while you make the icing. Put the icing ingredients in a small pan, heat and whisk until smooth. Cool for 20 minutes.

3 Flip the cooled cake on to a wire rack, flat-side up. Pour over the icing and leave to cool completely. Sprinkle with dark chocolate shavings (if using), then serve.

PER SERVING 276 kcals, protein 5g, carbs 39g, fat 11g, sat fat 2g, fibre 2g, sugar 26g, salt 0.5g

Chocca-mocca caramel cake

Scatter over a handful of little chocolate eggs for an Easter treat.

 1½ hours   10–12

- 175g/6oz butter, softened, plus extra for greasing
- 2 tsp instant coffee granules/powder
- 2 tbsp cocoa powder
- 175g/6oz golden caster sugar
- 2 eggs
- 2 tbsp golden syrup
- 200g/8oz self-raising flour
- 4 tbsp milk
- 2 x 50g chocolate caramel bars, broken into pieces

FOR THE ICING

- 2 x 50g chocolate caramel bars, broken into pieces
- 50g/2oz butter
- 2 tbsp milk
- 100g/4oz icing sugar, sifted

1 Heat oven to 180C/160C fan/gas 4. Butter and line the base of a 20cm-round cake tin. Mix the coffee, cocoa and 2 tablespoons hot water to a smooth paste. Put the butter, sugar, eggs, syrup, flour, milk and cocoa paste in a bowl, and beat for 2–3 minutes until smooth. Stir the caramel-bar pieces into the mixture.

2 Turn the mixture into the prepared tin and smooth. Bake for 50 minutes–1 hour, until the top springs back when you press it lightly. Cool in the tin for 5 minutes, then turn out, peel off the lining paper and leave to cool on a wire rack.

3 For the icing, gently heat the caramel-bar pieces, butter and milk until smooth, stirring all the time, then remove from the heat and stir in the icing sugar. Leave to cool. Spread the icing over the top of the cooled cake.

PER SERVING (10) 474 kcals, protein 5g, carbs 59g, fat 26g, sat fat 15g, fibre 1g, sugar 43g, salt 0.8g

Chocolate-gingerbread brownie bars with fudgy icing

These luxurious bars are based on a classic flourless cake, so they're rich and light in equal measure.

🕐 55 minutes   🥧 15

- 250g/9oz butter, plus extra for greasing
- 400g/14oz dark chocolate, broken into chunks
- 25g/1oz cocoa powder
- 250g/9oz golden caster sugar
- 1 tbsp ground ginger
- 140g/5oz ground almonds
- 6 eggs, separated

FOR THE ICING & DECORATION
- 100g/4oz butter, cubed
- 50g/2oz dark chocolate, use a bar broken into pieces or chips
- 50g/2oz cocoa powder
- 200g/7oz icing sugar, sifted
- 2 tbsp ground ginger
- few chunks crystallised ginger, chopped into small pieces

1 Heat oven to 180C/160C fan/gas 4. Grease a 20 x 30cm cake tin, and line the base and sides with baking parchment. Melt the chocolate, cocoa, sugar and butter together in a pan over a very low heat. Once melted, remove from the heat and stir in the ginger and almonds, followed by the egg yolks, one at a time.

2 In a clean bowl, beat the egg whites until stiff, then stir a couple of spoonfuls into the chocolate mixture. Very gently fold in the rest with a metal spoon.

3 Gently scrape the mixture into the tin. Bake for 30–35 minutes. Sit the tin on a wire rack and cool completely.

4 Put the butter, chocolate, cocoa, icing sugar, ground ginger and 4 tablespoons water in a pan. Gently heat, stirring, until smooth. Pour over the cake, leave for 1–2 minutes to cool slightly, then scatter over the ginger. Cool until set then cut into bars.

PER BAR 553 kcals, protein 7g, carbs 51g, fat 36g, sat fat 19g, fibre 2g, sugar 49g, salt 0.6g

Chunky chocolate-nut flapjacks

This flapjack, bulging with chunks of chocolate and nuts, is brilliant for lunchboxes.

 45 minutes 12

- 140g/5oz butter, cut into pieces, plus extra for greasing
- 200g/8oz oats
- 25g/1oz desiccated coconut
- 50g/2oz light muscovado sugar
- 5 tbsp golden syrup
- 100g/4oz brazil nuts (or cashew nuts), cut into large chunks
- 50g/2oz almonds, cut into large chunks
- 85g/3oz good-quality dark chocolate, broken into large pieces

1 Heat oven to 180C/160C fan/gas 4. Lightly butter a 23cm-square tin and line the base. Mix together the oats and coconut.

2 Put the butter, sugar and syrup in a pan, cook over a low heat, stirring occasionally, until the butter has melted and the sugar dissolved. Remove from the heat and stir in the oat-and-coconut mixture. Spoon into the tin and press down evenly. Scatter over the nuts and press lightly into the mixture. Stick the chunks of chocolate among the nuts. Bake for 25–30 minutes, or until a pale golden colour.

3 Mark into bars or squares with the back of a knife while still warm, then allow to cool completely before cutting through and removing from the tin.

PER FLAPJACK 325 kcals, protein 5g, carbs 28g, fat 22g, sat fat 10g, fibre 2g, sugar 15g, salt 0.3g

Banana–nut brownies

Deliciously moist, chocolatey and utterly irresistible – they'll keep for up to a week, tightly wrapped in foil.

🕐 50 minutes 🥧 15

- 175g/6oz butter, cut into pieces, plus extra for greasing
- 300g/10oz light muscovado sugar
- 175g/6oz dark chocolate, broken into pieces
- 100g bag nuts, toasted and chopped
- 3 eggs, beaten
- 2 ripe bananas, mashed
- 100g/4oz self-raising flour
- 2 tbsp cocoa powder
- 1 tsp baking powder

1 Heat oven to 180C/160C fan/gas 4. Butter and line an 18 x 28cm Swiss roll tin with baking paper. Put the butter, sugar and chocolate in a large pan, and heat gently, stirring, until melted and smooth, then remove the pan from the heat.

2 Stir in the nuts, eggs and bananas until well mixed, then sift in the flour, cocoa and baking powder.

3 Pour the mixture into the tin and bake for 30 minutes until firm in the centre. Cool in the tin, then turn out and cut into 15 squares.

PER BROWNIE 336 kcals, protein 5g, carbs 37g, fat 20g, sat fat 9g, fibre 1g, sugar 28g, salt 0.5g

Choc crunchies

This no-bake treat is great for lunchboxes.

🕐 50 minutes   🥧 8–10

- 100g/4oz butter, plus extra for greasing
- 200g/8oz digestive biscuits
- 3 tbsp golden syrup
- 2 tbsp cocoa powder
- 50g/2oz raisins
- 100g/4oz dark chocolate

1 Butter an 18cm sandwich tin. Seal the biscuits in a strong polythene bag and bash into uneven crumbs with a rolling pin.
2 Melt the butter and syrup in a pan (or microwave on High for about 1½ minutes). Stir in the cocoa and raisins, then thoroughly stir in the biscuit crumbs. Spoon into the tin and press down firmly.
3 Melt the chocolate in a heatproof bowl over a pan of simmering water (or microwave on Medium for 2–3 minutes). Spread over the biscuit base and chill for about half an hour. Keeps for up to 1 week wrapped in foil.

PER SERVING (8) 327 kcals, protein 3g, carbs 36g, fat 20g, sat fat 11g, fibre 1g, sugar 17g, salt 0.77g

Crispy chocolate fridge cake

Packed with biscuits, sultanas, puffed rice and lots of chocolate, these refrigerator bars are ideal for a kids' party

🕐 20 minutes, plus chilling   🍰 16-20

- 300g/11oz dark chocolate, broken into chunks
- 100g/4oz butter, diced
- 140g/5oz golden syrup
- 1 tsp vanilla extract
- 200g/7oz biscuits, roughly chopped
- 100g/4oz sultanas
- 85g/3oz Rice Krispies
- 100-140g/4-5oz mini eggs (optional)
- 50g/2oz white chocolate, melted

1 Line a 20 x 30cm tin with baking parchment. Melt the chocolate, butter and golden syrup in a bowl set over a pan of simmering water, stirring occasionally, until smooth and glossy. Add the vanilla, biscuits, sultanas and Rice Krispies, and mix until everything is coated.

2 Tip the mixture into the tin, then flatten it down with the back of a spoon. Press in some mini eggs, if using, and put in the fridge until set. When hard, drizzle all over with the melted white chocolate and set again before cutting into chunks.

PER CHUNK (20) Kcals 249, protein 2g, carbs 32g, fat 12g, sat fat 7g, fibre 1g, sugar 24g, salt 0.4g

Cappuccino bars

These moreish bars can be frozen, unfrosted, for up to 2 months.

 50 minutes   24

- 200g/8oz butter, softened, plus extra for greasing
- 1 tsp cocoa powder, plus extra for dusting
- 2 rounded tbsp coffee granules
- 200g/8oz caster sugar
- 4 eggs
- 200g/8oz self-raising flour
- 1 tsp baking powder

FOR THE WHITE-CHOCOLATE FROSTING

- 100g/4oz white chocolate, broken into pieces
- 50g/2oz butter, softened
- 3 tbsp milk
- 175g/6oz icing sugar

1 Heat oven to 180C/160C fan/gas 4. Butter and line the bottom of a shallow 28 x 18cm oblong tin. Mix the cocoa and coffee granules into 2 tablespoons warm water. Put in a large bowl with the other cake ingredients.

2 Whisk for about 2 minutes with an electric hand blender to combine, then tip into the tin and level out. Bake for 35–40 minutes until risen and firm to the touch. Cool in the tin for 10 minutes, then cool completely on a wire rack. Peel off the paper.

3 For the frosting, melt the chocolate, butter and milk in a bowl over a pan of simmering water. Remove the bowl and sift in the icing sugar. Beat until smooth, then spread over the cake. Finish with a dusting of cocoa powder. Cut into 24 bars.

Toffee brownies

Unrefined dark muscovado sugar gives these brownies a sticky toffee flavour.

🕐 1 hour 5 minutes, plus 1 hour cooling   🥧 16

- 250g/9oz unsalted butter, cut into pieces, plus extra for greasing
- 350g/12oz dark chocolate (preferably 50–60% cocoa solids), broken into pieces
- 3 eggs
- 250g/9oz dark muscovado sugar
- 85g/3oz plain flour
- 1 tsp baking powder

1 Heat oven to 160C/140C fan/gas 3. Butter and line the base of a shallow 23cm -square cake tin. Melt the chocolate and butter together in a small pan, then stir well and cool.

2 Whisk the eggs in a large bowl until pale, then whisk in the sugar until thick and glossy and well combined. Gently fold in the melted-chocolate mixture, then sift in the flour and baking powder, and gently stir until smooth.

3 Pour into the prepared cake tin and bake for 30–35 minutes or until firm to the touch. Test by inserting a wooden cocktail stick into the middle of the brownie – there should be a few moist crumbs sticking to it. The mixture will still be soft in the centre, but will firm up on cooling.

4 Cool in the tin on a wire rack for at least 1 hour, then cut into 16 squares and finish cooling on the rack.

PER BROWNIE 324 kcals, protein 3g, carbs 34g, fat 20g, sat fat 12g, fibre 1g, sugar 30g, salt 0.14g

Mincemeat & marzipan tea bread

A treat for tea by the fire, this afternoon bake keeps moist, well-wrapped, for 4–5 days.

🕐 1 hour 20 minutes 12

- 100g/4oz cold butter, cut into pieces, plus extra for greasing
- 200g/8oz self-raising flour
- 85g/3oz light muscovado sugar
- 85g/3oz marzipan, cut into 1cm/½in cubes
- 2 eggs
- 300g/10oz mincemeat
- 2 tbsp flaked almonds
- icing sugar, for dusting (optional)

1 Heat oven to 180C/160C fan/gas 4. Butter a 1kg loaf tin and line the base with greaseproof paper. Tip the flour into a bowl, add the cold butter and rub until the mixture forms fine crumbs. Stir in the sugar and marzipan cubes.

2 In another bowl, lightly whisk the eggs, then stir in the mincemeat. Stir this into the flour mixture until evenly combined. Spoon into the prepared loaf tin, smooth, and sprinkle the flaked almonds over the top. Bake for 1 hour until the tea bread is risen and golden brown, or a skewer inserted into the centre of the cake comes out clean. Lightly dust the tea bread with icing sugar while it is still hot.

3 Allow to cool in the tin for 10 minutes, then tip on to a wire rack to cool completely. Peel off the lining paper and cut into slices – it's also very good spread with butter.

PER SERVING 265 kcals, protein 4g, carbs 41g, fat 11g, sat fat 5g, fibre 1g, sugar 15g, salt 0.44g

Banana tea bread

The natural sweetness provided by the bananas helps reduce the amount of sugar that needs to be used.

 1 hour 35 minutes 🥧 10

- 100g/4oz butter, softened, plus extra for greasing
- 175g/6oz plain wholemeal flour
- 50g/2oz medium oatmeal
- 100g/4oz dark muscovado sugar
- 2 tsp baking powder
- ¼ tsp ground cinnamon
- 2 eggs, beaten
- 3–4 ripe bananas, about 350g/12oz total, peeled and mashed
- 100g/4oz walnuts, roughly chopped

1 Heat oven to 180C/160C fan/gas 4. Butter and line the base of a 1kg loaf tin with baking paper. Put the wholemeal flour, oatmeal, butter, sugar, baking powder, cinnamon and eggs into a large bowl and, using an electric hand whisk, beat together until evenly mixed. Stir in the bananas and walnuts, taking care not to overmix.

2 Spoon the mixture into the prepared tin and bake for 1¼ hours or until a skewer inserted into the centre of the cake comes out clean (cover the cake with foil halfway through cooking to prevent the top from overbrowning). Allow the cake to cool in the tin for 5 minutes, then carefully turn out, peel off the lining paper and cool completely on a wire rack.

PER SERVING 309 kcals, protein 6g, carbs 34g, fat 17g, sat fat 3g, fibre 3g, sugar 10g, salt 0.53g

Walnut, date & honey cake

Choose a richly flavoured Greek or Mexican honey for an extra-special taste.

 1 hour 25 minutes   8–10

- 175g/6oz butter, softened, plus extra for greasing
- 200g/8oz self-raising flour
- ½ tsp ground cinnamon
- 100g/4oz light muscovado sugar
- 3 tbsp clear honey
- 2 eggs, beaten
- 2 ripe medium bananas, about 250g/9oz total in their skins
- 100g/4oz stoned dates
- 50g pack walnut pieces

1 Heat oven to 160C/140C fan/gas 3. Line the base and long sides of a 1kg loaf tin with greaseproof paper, buttering the tin and paper. Tip the flour, cinnamon, butter, sugar, 2 tablespoons of the honey and the eggs into a large mixing bowl. Mash the bananas and chop the dates (kitchen scissors are easiest for this), and add to the bowl. Beat the mixture for 2–3 minutes, using a wooden spoon or hand-held mixer, until well blended.

2 Spoon into the prepared tin and smooth. Scatter the walnut pieces over the top. Bake for 1 hour, then lightly press the top – it should feel firm. If not, bake for a further 10 minutes.

3 Cool for 15 minutes, then lift out of the tin using the paper. When cold, drizzle over the remaining honey. Cut into thick slices.

PER SERVING (8) 440 kcals, protein 6g, carbs 54g, fat 24g, sat fat 13g, fibre 2g, sugar 25g, salt 0.7g

Lovely lemon-drizzle loaf

. . . .

A classic recipe for this much-loved citrus sponge with its crunchy sugar topping and moist texture.

🕐 1 hour 10 minutes   🍽 10

- 200g/8oz salted butter, softened, plus a little for greasing
- 200g/8oz golden caster sugar
- zest 3 large unwaxed lemons (save a little to decorate)
- 3 eggs, at room temperature
- 200g/8oz self-raising flour
- 50g/2oz full-fat natural yogurt
- 2 tbsp good-quality lemon curd

FOR THE DRIZZLE
- juice 1½ lemons
- 85g/3oz granulated sugar
- 4–5 sugar cubes, crushed

1 Heat oven to 170C/150C fan/gas 3½. Grease a 1kg loaf tin and line with baking parchment. Put the butter, caster sugar and lemon zest in a large bowl and beat with an electric hand whisk until pale and fluffy. Crack in 1 of the eggs, whisk into the butter mixture until well combined, then add 1 heaped tablespoon of the flour and mix again. Continue with the remaining eggs and flour until combined. Fold in the yogurt and lemon curd with a spatula until smooth.

2 Scrape the mixture into the tin and bake in the centre of the oven for 45–50 minutes until golden and risen – a skewer inserted into the centre of the cake should come out clean. Leave to cool in the tin for 5 minutes.

3 For the drizzle, mix the lemon juice and sugars in a small bowl. Transfer the cake to a cooling rack. Using a fine skewer or cocktail stick, poke holes all over the top of the cake. Spoon over the drizzle, scatter with the reserved zest and leave to soak in for 10 minutes before serving. Will keep in a cake tin for 3 days.

. . . .

PER SERVING 377 kcals, protein 4g, carbs 49g, fat 19g, sat fat 11g, fibre 1g, sugar 32g, salt 0.6g

Toffee-apple & pecan loaf

Apples and caramel are a heavenly duo. This nutty sandwich loaf with buttercream frosting and caramel drizzle fits the bill nicely.

🕐 1¼ hours   🥧 10

- 175g/6oz unsalted butter, softened, plus extra for greasing
- 200g/8oz Carnation caramel
- 50g/2oz light muscovado sugar
- 3 eggs, at room temperature
- 175g/6oz plain flour
- 1 tsp baking powder
- 1 tsp vanilla extract
- 1 tangy eating apple, peeled, ½ chopped, ½ thinly sliced
- 50g/2oz pecan nuts, ½ finely chopped, ½ roughly broken

FOR THE FROSTING & DRIZZLE
- 50g/2oz icing sugar
- 25g/1oz unsalted butter, just softened but not greasy
- 2 tbsp Carnation caramel

1 Grease a 1kg loaf tin and line with a strip of baking parchment. Heat oven to 180C/160C fan/gas 4. Using electric hand beaters, beat the caramel, sugar and butter until smooth and even. Add the eggs, flour, baking powder and vanilla, then beat again until even. Fold in the chopped apples and chopped pecans.

2 Spoon the mix into the loaf tin, poke the sliced apples into the mix and scatter over the broken pecans. Bake for 30 minutes, then cover the top loosely with foil and return to the oven for 30 minutes more, until risen and a skewer inserted into the middle of the cake comes out clean. Cool for 10 minutes in the tin; transfer to a wire rack to cool completely.

3 For the frosting, cream the icing sugar and butter together with electric beaters until pale, then beat in 1 tablespoon of the caramel. Split the cake in two and sandwich with the frosting. To finish, warm the remaining caramel with 1 teaspoon water until runny, then drizzle over the cake.

PER SERVING 340 kcals, protein 5g, carbs 30g, fat 22g, sat fat 12g, fibre 1g, sugar 18g, salt 0.2g

Sticky marmalade tea loaf

· ·

Use a chunky marmalade to give this loaf extra texture and a pretty top.

🕐 1½ hours   🥧 12

- 175g/6oz butter, softened, plus extra for greasing
- 140g/5oz marmalade (about one-third x 454g jar)
- 175g/6oz light muscovado sugar
- 3 eggs, beaten
- 200g/8oz self-raising flour
- ½ tsp baking powder
- 2 tsp ground ginger
- 1 tsp ground mixed spice
- 100g packet pecan nut halves

1 Heat oven to 180C/160C fan/gas 4/ Butter a 1kg loaf tin and line with greaseproof paper. Set aside 1 tablespoon of the marmalade in a small pan. In a bowl, blend the remaining marmalade, the butter, sugar, eggs, flour, baking powder and spices for 1–2 minutes until smooth and light. Stir in about three-quarters of the pecans.

2 Tip into the prepared tin and smooth the top. Sprinkle with the reserved pecans. Bake for about 1–1¼ hours until a skewer inserted in the centre of the cake comes out clean. Cover loosely with foil after 40 minutes. Once cooked, carefully remove from the tin, and cool slightly on a wire rack.

3 Gently heat the reserved marmalade, stirring until it's smooth, and spread the glaze over the top of the warm loaf. Serve in slices.

· ·
PER SERVING 339 kcals, protein 4g, carbs 40g, fat 20g, sat fat 8g, fibre 1g, sugar 24g, salt 0.56g

Cherry chocolate Bakewell cake

. . . .

An irresistible almond sponge, studded with juicy cherries and chocolate chunks, that'll keep in your cake tin for a few days - if it lasts that long!

🕐 1 hour 35 minutes   🍰 8-10

- 200g/7oz butter, softened, plus extra for greasing
- 140g/5oz fresh cherries, halved and stoned
- 140g/5oz plain flour
- 200g/7oz golden caster sugar
- 3 eggs
- 1½ tsp baking powder
- 75g/2 ½ oz ground almonds
- 2 tbsp milk
- 1 tsp vanilla extract
- 1 tsp almond extract
- 200g/7oz dark or milk chocolate, chopped
- 2 tbsp toasted flaked almonds

1 Heat oven to 160C/140C fan/gas 3. Grease and line a 900g loaf tin with baking parchment. Toss the cherries in 1 tbsp of the flour, then set aside.

2 Put the butter and sugar in a large bowl, and whisk until light and fluffy. Add the eggs, 1 at a time, mixing well between each addition. Fold in the remaining flour, the baking powder and ground almonds. Stir in the milk, the vanilla and almond extracts, and 100g of the chocolate with a spatula. Scrape half the cake mixture into the tin, scatter half the cherries over the top, then add the remaining cake mixture and the remaining cherries. Bake for 1 hour 10 minutes or until a skewer comes out clean.

3 Cool in the tin for 10 minutes, then remove to a wire rack to cool completely. Melt the remaining chocolate in the microwave in 20-second bursts, then drizzle or pipe over the top of the cake and scatter with the almonds. Let the chocolate set a bit before slicing. Will keep in the cake tin for up to 4 days.

. . . .

PER SLICE (10) Kcals 490, protein 7g, carbs 42g, fat 32g, sat fat 16g, fibre 2g, sugar 30g, salt 0.6g

Date & walnut tea loaf

· ·

Although a fast and easy recipe for tea, this loaf is best made a day or two in advance.

 1 hour 40 minutes, plus cooling   10–12

- 200g/8oz stoned dates, chopped
- 1 tsp bicarbonate of soda
- 100g/4oz butter, cut into pieces, plus extra for greasing
- 300g/10oz self-raising flour, sifted
- 50g/2oz chopped walnuts
- 100g/4oz dark muscovado sugar
- 1 egg, beaten
- 2 tbsp demerara sugar

1 Mix the dates and bicarbonate of soda in a large bowl with a pinch of salt. Pour in 300ml/½ pint hot water, stir well and leave until cold. Heat oven to 180C/160C fan/gas 4. Butter a 1kg loaf tin and line the base and two long sides.

2 Rub the butter pieces into the flour until the mixture resembles coarse breadcrumbs. Stir in the walnuts and muscovado sugar until evenly combined.

3 Tip the flour mixture and the egg into the cooled dates. Beat well to mix, then pour into the prepared tin and sprinkle the demerara sugar on top. Bake in the oven for 1–1¼ hours or until a skewer inserted into the centre of the loaf comes out clean. Cool in the tin for 5 minutes, then turn out on to a wire rack. Double-wrap the cooled cake and store in an airtight tin for 1–2 days.

· ·

PER SERVING (10) 317 kcals, protein 5g, carbs 49g, fat 13g, sat fat 6g, fibre 2g, sugar 14g, salt 0.9g

Pumpkin & ginger tea bread

The pumpkin adds a depth of flavour, a certain sweetness and a lusciously moist texture.

 1½ hours 10

- 175g/6oz butter, melted, plus extra to grease
- 140g/5oz clear honey
- 1 egg, beaten
- 250g/9oz raw peeled pumpkin or butternut squash, deseeded and coarsely grated (about 500g/1lb 2oz total before peeling and deseeding)
- 100g/4oz light muscovado sugar
- 350g/12oz self-raising flour
- 1 tbsp ground ginger
- 2 tbsp demerara sugar, plus extra for sprinkling (optional)

1 Heat oven to 180C/160C fan/gas 4. Butter and line the base and two long sides of a 1kg loaf tin with a strip of baking paper.
2 Mix the butter, honey and egg, and stir in the pumpkin or squash. Then mix in the sugar, flour and ginger.
3 Pour into the prepared tin and sprinkle the top with the demerara sugar. Bake for 50 minutes–1 hour, until risen and golden brown. Leave in the tin for 5 minutes, then turn out and cool on a wire rack. Sprinkle more demerara sugar over the warm cake, if you wish. Serve thickly sliced.

PER SERVING 351 kcals, protein 4g, carbs 52g, fat 15g, sat fat 9g, fibre 1g, sugar 24g, salt 0.69g

Blackberry & apple loaf

Try other fruits when in season – raspberries and tayberries would be good.

🕐 2 hours 🥧 10

- 175g/6oz butter, plus extra for greasing
- 250g/9oz self-raising flour
- 175g/6oz light muscovado sugar
- ½ tsp ground cinnamon
- 2 rounded tbsp demerara sugar
- 1 small eating apple, unpeeled, coarsely grated down to the core
- 2 eggs, beaten
- finely grated zest 1 orange
- 1 tsp baking powder
- 200g/8oz blackberries

1 Heat oven to 180C/160C fan/gas 4. Butter and line the base of a 1kg loaf tin. Rub the flour, butter and muscovado sugar together to make fine crumbs. Reserve 5 tablespoons of this mixture for the topping, and mix into it the cinnamon and demerara sugar. Set aside.

2 Mix the apple in with the eggs and zest. Stir the baking powder into the rubbed-in mixture, then quickly and lightly stir in the egg mixture. Don't overmix.

3 Gently fold in three-quarters of the berries. Spoon into the tin and level. Scatter the rest of the berries on top. Sprinkle over the reserved topping and bake for 1 hour 20 minutes, testing with a skewer. After 50 minutes, cover loosely with foil. Leave in the tin for 30 minutes, then cool on a wire rack.

PER SERVING 327 kcals, protein 4g, carbs 44g, fat 16g, sat fat 10g, fibre 2g, sugar 23g, salt 0.77g

Banana & walnut tea loaf

• •

Sealed in a plastic food bag, this loaf will freeze for up to 3 months.

🕐 1¼ hours   🍰 12

- 100g/4oz butter, softened, plus extra for greasing
- 140g/5oz light muscovado sugar
- 2 eggs, lightly beaten
- 100g/4oz walnuts, chopped
- 2 ripe bananas, mashed
- 2 tbsp milk
- 200g/8oz self-raising flour

1 Heat oven to 180C/160C fan/gas 4. Butter and line a 1kg loaf tin. Cream the butter and sugar, then add the eggs. Set aside 25g/1oz walnuts, then fold the rest into the creamed mixture with the bananas and milk. Fold in the flour. Spoon into the tin and sprinkle over the reserved walnuts.

2 Bake for 55 minutes–1 hour until risen. Stand for 10 minutes, then turn out, remove the lining paper and cool.

• •

PER SERVING 267 kcals, protein 4g, carbs 33g, fat 14g, sat fat 5g, fibre 1g, sugar 12g, salt 0.37g

Shortbread

· · · · · · · · · · · · · · · · · · · ·

Unrefined caster sugar and a salted or slightly salted creamy butter will give the best flavour.

🕐 50 minutes   🍰 8

- 150g/6oz plain flour, plus extra for dusting
- 100g/4oz slightly salted butter, cut into pieces and softened
- 50g/2oz golden caster sugar
- caster sugar, for sprinkling

1 Heat oven to 150C/130C fan/gas 2. Put the flour in a mixing bowl, add the butter and rub together to make fine crumbs. Stir in the sugar.

2 Work the mixture together until it forms a ball. Turn out on to a work surface and knead briefly until smooth. Roll and pat out on a very lightly floured surface to an 18cm/7in round. Smooth the surface with your hands. Carefully slide the dough on to an ungreased baking sheet and flute the edges. Mark the circle into eight triangles with a knife, not cutting all the way through. Prick the surface all over with a fork.

3 Bake for 30–35 minutes or until cooked. The shortbread should be very pale. While still warm, cut through the markings and sprinkle with caster sugar. Cool before eating.

· · · · · · · · · · · · · · · · · · · ·

PER SERVING 186 kcals, protein 2g, carbs 22g, fat 10g, sat fat 7g, fibre 1g, sugar 8g, salt trace

Buttermilk scones

Buttermilk adds a lightness that milk alone won't give you.

 25 minutes 12

- 350g/12oz self-raising flour, plus extra for dusting
- 100g/4oz caster sugar
- 85g/3oz cold butter, cut into small pieces
- about 175ml/6fl oz buttermilk or natural low-fat yogurt
- whipped cream and strawberry jam, to serve

1 Heat oven to 200C/180C fan/gas 6. Mix together the flour and sugar in a bowl. Rub the butter in with your fingertips until the mixture resembles fine breadcrumbs. Make a well in the centre of the ingredients and tip in the buttermilk, all in one go, then mix lightly to form a soft dough.

2 Tip the dough out on to a lightly floured surface and knead briefly. Press the dough out to a 2.5cm/1in thickness, then stamp out 5cm/2in rounds with a cutter. Gather up the trimmings, knead again briefly and stamp out more rounds.

3 Transfer the buttermilk scones to a baking sheet, spaced a little apart, and bake for 12–15 minutes until risen and light golden. Leave the scones to cool on a wire rack and serve with the whipped cream and jam.

PER SCONE 187 kcals, protein 3g, carbs 32g, fat 6g, sat fat 4g, fibre 1g, sugar 9g, salt 0.42g

Caramel-button cupcakes

These individual sponges have a secret centre and a soft cheese frosting. Serve topped with homemade caramel buttons.

🕐 50 minutes   🥧 12

- 175g/6oz butter, softened
- 175g/6oz light muscovado sugar
- 2 eggs
- 175g/6oz self-raising flour
- 2 tbsp milk

FOR THE ICING
- 397g can Carnation caramel
- 200g tub full-fat soft cheese
- 100g/4oz salted butter, softened
- 450g/15oz golden icing sugar

FOR THE CARAMEL BUTTONS
- 2 x 30g Caramac bars
- 10 soft toffees
- splash milk

1 Heat oven to 180C/160C fan/gas 4. Line a 12-hole muffin tin with cases. Using an electric whisk, cream the butter and sugar until smooth. Add the eggs and whisk again, then add the flour and milk, and mix with a spatula until well combined. Divide the mixture among the cases. Bake for 18–20 minutes until springy. Leave to cool.

2 Meanwhile, make the caramel buttons. Put the bars in a bowl and melt in short blasts in the microwave on High, stirring every 20 seconds. Gently melt the toffees in a pan with the milk. Transfer to a piping bag. Line a baking sheet with baking parchment and spoon on small blobs of the melted bars. Pipe the toffee sauce over the discs. Leave to set.

3 Make the icing. Mix 140g of the caramel with the other ingredients with an electric hand whisk, until smooth. Chill for 10 minutes.

4 Cut a hole in the centre of each cake and fill with the remaining Caramel. Transfer the icing to a piping bag and swirl over the tops, then decorate with the caramel buttons.

PER CUPCAKE 667 kcals, protein 5g, carbs 87g, fat 33g, sat fat 21g, fibre 1g, sugar 76g, salt 0.8g

Orange & almond cupcakes

. . . .

Delicate little cupcakes with almond buttercream icing swirled into a pretty rose design.

 1 hour 55 minutes   🕐 24

- 300g/11oz butter, softened
- 300g/11oz golden caster sugar
- 4 eggs
- 250g/9oz plain flour
- 100g/4oz ground almonds
- 2½ tsp baking powder
- zest 1 orange, plus 2 tbsp juice
- 1 tsp almond extract

FOR THE BUTTERCREAM ICING

- 200g/7oz butter, softened
- 450g/1lb icing sugar, plus a little extra
- 200g/7oz cream cheese
- 1 tsp almond extract
- 1 tbsp orange juice
- food colouring paste of your choice (we used a mixture of pink and yellow to create coral)
- 250g pack green sugar paste (or fondant icing mixed with green food colouring)

1 Heat oven to 170C/150C fan/gas 3½. Line 2 x 12-hole muffin tins with muffin cases. Blend the butter and caster sugar in a large bowl with an electric hand whisk until pale and fluffy. Add the eggs, one at a time, whisking well. Add the flour, almonds, baking powder and a pinch of salt. Mix again, then add the orange zest and juice, and almond extract. Give a final mix to combine everything.

2 Divide the mixture between the cases. Bake for 22-25 minutes, changing the tins over after 15 minutes. Remove from the oven, leave for 10 minutes in the tins, then transfer to a wire rack to cool completely.

3 To make the icing, blend the butter in a large bowl with an electric hand whisk until smooth. Add the icing sugar, cream cheese, almond extract and orange juice and whisk until smooth. Add the food colouring and mix again until you have an even colour.

4 Using a large curved star point nozzle, Pipe a swirl on top of each cake with a piping bag.

5 Before serving, shape small pieces of green sugar paste into leaves and use to decorate.

. . . .

PER CUPCAKE Kcals 428, protein 3g, carbs 48g, fat 25g, sat fat 14g, fibre g, sugar 41g, salt 0.6g

Easter nest coconut & white-chocolate cupcakes

. . . .

Try saying no to these little frosted sponges with their clever bird decorations made with chocolate eggs.

🕐 1 hour   🥧 12

- 3 medium eggs, beaten
- 100ml/3½fl oz milk
- 1 tsp vanilla extract
- 175g/6oz golden caster sugar
- 100g/4oz desiccated coconut
- 200g/8oz self-raising flour
- 50g/2oz melted butter
- 100g/4oz white chocolate, melted

FOR THE FROSTING
- 100g/4oz white chocolate, melted
- 200g/8oz unsalted butter, at room temperature
- 200g/8oz icing sugar, sifted

TO DECORATE
- about 25g/1oz shredded coconut
- orange icing, for beaks
- 36 mini eggs
- black writing icing tube

1 Heat oven to 180C/160C fan/gas 4. Line a 12-hole muffin tin with paper cases. Whisk together the eggs, milk and vanilla. Whizz the sugar with the coconut in a food processor until finely ground. Tip into a mixing bowl with the flour and mix. Stir together with the egg mixture, butter and chocolate, until smooth.

2 Spoon into the cases. Bake for 18–20 minutes until golden. Cool on a wire rack.

3 Spread the shredded coconut on a baking sheet and lightly toast in the oven for about 10 minutes – stir halfway through. Cool.

4 To make the frosting, combine the chocolate, butter and icing sugar in a bowl using an electric whisk, then spread some over the cooled cakes. Use the remaining icing to pipe around the edge of the cakes to make a nest. Gently press in the cooled coconut to coat.

5 Mould beaks from the orange icing and stick on each egg with black icing. Pipe on black eyes. Stick chicks into the middle of each cake.

. . . .

PER CUPCAKE 499 kcals, protein 5g, carbs 56g, fat 29g, sat fat 19g, fibre 2g, sugar 44g, salt 0.3g

Lemon & violet drizzle squares

• •

This all-in-one cake mixes easily, keeps for a week wrapped in foil and freezes well.

 1 hour   15

- 100g/4oz butter, softened, plus extra for greasing
- 175g/6oz self-raising flour
- 1 tsp baking powder
- 175g/6oz golden caster sugar
- 2 eggs
- 6 tbsp milk
- finely grated rind 1 large lemon

FOR THE ICING & DECORATION
- juice 1 large lemon (you need 3 tablespoons)
- 100g/4oz golden caster sugar
- crystallised violets and mimosa balls (or yellow sugar balls)

1 Heat oven to 180C/160C fan/gas 4. Butter and line the base of a shallow oblong tin (about 18 x 28cm) with baking paper. Tip all the cake ingredients into a large mixing bowl and beat for 2–3 minutes, until the mixture drops easily off the spoon.

2 Spoon the mixture into the prepared tin and smooth the surface with the back of a spoon. Bake for 30–40 minutes, until golden and firm to the touch. Meanwhile, make the icing: beat together the lemon juice and sugar, pour the mixture evenly over the cake while it is still hot, then leave to cool.

3 Cut the cake into 15 squares. Top each one with a crystallised violet and mimosa ball.

• •
PER SQUARE 175 kcals, protein 2g, carbs 29g, fat 7g, sat fat 4g, fibre none, sugar 19g, salt 0.3g

Blueberry & lemon friands

These light-as-air cakes are sold in every self-respecting coffee shop in Sydney – try them and you too will be hooked.

 40 minutes   6

- 100g/4oz unsalted butter, plus extra for greasing
- 125g/4½oz icing sugar, plus extra for dusting
- 25g/1oz plain flour
- 85g/3oz ground almonds
- 3 egg whites
- grated rind 1 unwaxed lemon
- 85g/3oz blueberries

1 Heat oven to 200C/180C fan/gas 6. Generously butter six non-stick friand or muffin tins. Melt the butter and set aside to cool.

2 Sift the icing sugar and flour into a bowl. Add the almonds and mix everything between your fingers. Whisk the egg whites in another bowl until they form a light, floppy foam. Make a well in the centre of the dry ingredients, tip in the egg whites and lemon rind, then lightly stir in the butter to form a soft batter.

3 Divide the batter among the tins (a large serving spoon is perfect for this job). Sprinkle a handful of blueberries over each cake and bake for 15–20 minutes until just firm to the touch and golden brown. Cool in the tins for 5 minutes, then turn out and cool on a wire rack. To serve, dust lightly with icing sugar.

PER FRIAND 316 kcals, protein 5g, carbs 27g, fat 22g, sat fat 9g, fibre 1g, sugar 22g, salt 0.09g

Coconut & mango traybake

This thrifty traybake sponge uses canned fruit and coconut yogurt. Delicious served warm with an extra blob of coconut yogurt, but it is just as good cold

🕐 50 minutes   🥧 12

- 200g/8oz butter, softened, plus extra for greasing
- 425g can sliced mangoes in syrup, drained
- 200g/8oz golden caster sugar
- 4 eggs
- 200g/8oz self-raising flour
- 50g/2oz desiccated coconut, plus 3 tbsp for sprinkling
- 140g/5oz Greek-style coconut yogurt

1 Heat oven to 180C/160C fan/gas 4. Grease and line a 20 x 30cm baking tin with two strips of criss-crossed baking parchment. Dry the mango pieces on some kitchen paper, then chop into 2.5cm/1in pieces.

2 Put the butter and sugar into a bowl, and whisk until smooth and creamy. Add the eggs, one at a time, beating well after each addition. Use a spatula to fold through the flour and coconut, then the mango pieces and yogurt.

3 Scrape the mixture into the tin and smooth over the surface, then sprinkle with the extra coconut. Bake for 30 minutes until risen and golden and a skewer inserted into the centre of the cake comes out clean. Cool for 10 minutes in the tin, then transfer to a wire rack. Keeps in a tin for up to 3 days.

PER SERVING 360 kcals, protein 5g, carbs 36g, fat 22g, sat fat 14g, fibre 3g, sugar 24g, salt 0.5g

Apricot crumb squares

Ideal with a cup of tea at home, or to enjoy at your next picnic.

🕐 1¼ hours   ◖ 16

- 175g/6oz butter, softened, plus extra for greasing
- 200g/8oz golden caster sugar
- 3 eggs
- 175g/6oz plain flour
- 1 tsp baking powder
- 2–3 tbsp milk
- 8 fresh apricots (or canned in natural juice), quartered
- icing sugar, for dusting

FOR THE TOPPING

- 175g/6oz plain flour
- 140g/5oz light muscovado sugar
- 140g/5oz butter, softened
- 1 tsp ground cinnamon
- ½ tsp salt

1 Heat oven to 180C/160C fan/gas 4. Butter a shallow 23cm-square cake tin. To make the topping, put all of the topping ingredients in a food processor and blend to make a sticky crumble.

2 In a separate bowl, blend the butter, sugar, eggs, flour and baking powder using an electric hand whisk or wooden spoon, gradually adding enough milk to make a creamy mixture that drops from a spoon. Spread in the tin and scatter with apricots. Top with the crumble and press down.

3 Bake for 45–50 minutes until golden and a skewer inserted into the middle comes out clean. Cool in the tin, cut into 16 squares and dust with icing sugar.

PER SQUARE 332 kcals, protein 4g, carbs 42g, fat 18g, sat fat 11g, fibre 1g, sugar 22g, salt 0.52g

Blackcurrant crumble squares

· · · · · · · · · · · · · · · · · · · ·

These moist but crumbly squares are best eaten on the day, but will freeze for up to 3 months.

 1 hour   12

- 100g/4oz butter, softened, plus extra for greasing
- 175g/6oz caster sugar
- 1 egg
- 300g/10oz self-raising flour
- 125ml/4fl oz milk
- 200g/8oz fresh blackcurrants, destalked

FOR THE CRUMBLE
- 100g/4oz caster sugar
- 85g/3oz plain flour
- finely grated rind 1 lemon
- 50g/2oz cold butter

1 Heat oven to 180C/160C fan/gas 4. Butter a 28 x 18cm oblong cake tin and line with baking paper. (You could also use a 23cm-square tin or a 25cm-round tin.)

2 Beat the butter and sugar in a large bowl with an electric hand whisk until the mixture is pale and fluffy. Whisk in the egg, then carefully fold in the flour and milk until thoroughly combined. Spoon into the tin and spread evenly. Sprinkle over the blackcurrants.

3 Mix together the sugar, flour and lemon rind for the crumble. Rub in the butter until the mixture is crumbly, then sprinkle on top of the squares. Bake for 45 minutes until the topping is golden and the blackcurrants start to burst through; leave to cool in the tin. When cool, lift the cake out of the tin, and cut into squares.

· ·

PER SQUARE 315 kcals, protein 4g, carbs 50g, fat 13g, sat fat 8g, fibre 2g, sugar 25g, salt 0.29g

Spider-web chocolate fudge muffins

Light and chocolatey, these are the perfect Hallowe'en treat.

 50 minutes 10

- 50g/2oz dark chocolate, broken into pieces
- 85g/3oz butter
- 1 tbsp milk
- 200g/8oz self-raising flour
- ½ tsp bicarbonate of soda
- 85g/3oz light muscovado sugar
- 50g/2oz golden caster sugar
- 1 egg
- 142ml pot soured cream

FOR THE TOPPING
- 100g/4oz dark chocolate, broken into pieces and melted
- 100g/4oz white chocolate, broken into pieces and melted

1 Heat oven to 190C/170C fan/gas 5 and line a muffin tin with 10 paper cases. Heat the chocolate and butter in a pan with the milk until melted. Stir and cool.

2 Mix the flour, bicarbonate of soda and both sugars in a large bowl. Beat the egg in another bowl and stir in the soured cream, then pour this on the flour mixture and add the cooled chocolate. Stir just to combine – don't overmix. Spoon into the cases to about three-quarters full. Bake for 20 minutes until well risen. Cool in the tins for a few minutes, then lift out of the tins and continue to cool on a wire rack.

3 Spread one muffin with the dark chocolate for the topping, then pipe four circles of the white chocolate on top. Drag a skewer from the centre to the edge to create a cobweb effect. Alternate dark chocolate on white for the opposite effect.

PER MUFFFIN 349 kcals, protein 5g, carbs 45g, fat 18g, sat fat 9g, fibre 1g, sugar 28g, salt 0.59g

Festive mince pies

Top with marzipan stars or meringue before baking to vary this festive recipe.

🕐 40 minutes, plus 30 minutes chilling   🥧 18

FOR THE PASTRY
- 200g/8oz plain flour
- 50g/2oz ground almonds
- 140g/5oz butter, chopped into small pieces
- grated zest 1 orange
- 50g/2oz caster sugar
- 1 egg yolk

FOR THE FILLING & DECORATION
- 200g/8oz mincemeat
- 1 egg white, lightly whisked
- caster sugar, for dusting

1 Heat oven to 200C/180C fan/gas 6. Whizz the flour, almonds, butter, orange zest and sugar for the pastry into crumbs. Add the egg yolk and 1 teaspoon cold water, and pulse until it forms a dough. Wrap in cling film and chill for 30 minutes.

2 Roll out the dough thinly and stamp out eighteen 7.5cm/3in rounds. Use to line bun tins. Put 1 heaped teaspoon of the mincemeat in each pastry case. Stamp out nine more pastry rounds. Cut out festive shapes from the centre of each round.

3 Cover the pies with the shapes and pastry rounds with the centres removed. Brush the tops with egg white and dust lightly with caster sugar. Bake for 12–15 minutes until the pastry is crisp and golden. Cool in the tins for 5 minutes, then on a wire rack.

PER MINCE PIE 164 kcals, protein 2g, carbs 20g, fat 9g, sat fat 5g, fibre 1g, sugar 9g, salt 0.17g

Oaty plum-gingerbread squares

A rustic traybake for any time of day. Try a slice with coffee or with a jug of steaming custard for dessert.

 50 minutes   12

- 140g/5oz unsalted butter, plus extra for greasing
- 100g/4oz dark soft brown sugar
- 100g/4oz golden syrup
- 6 small plums (about 250g/9oz total prepared weight)
- 140g/5oz plain flour
- 1 tsp baking powder
- 1 tbsp ground ginger
- 1 heaped tbsp chopped stem ginger
- 85g/3oz porridge oats (not jumbo)
- 2 eggs, beaten, at room temperature

FOR THE TOPPING

- 25g/1oz plain flour
- 25g/1oz porridge oats
- 2 heaped tsp chopped ginger

1 Grease a 17 x 23cm cake tin and line with baking parchment. Heat oven to 180C/160C fan/gas 4. Melt the butter, sugar and syrup together in a large pan. While you wait, stone and quarter the plums.

2 When the pan ingredients are smooth, stir in the flour, baking powder, ¼ tsp salt, the gingers, oats and eggs, then beat until even. Pour all but about 2 tablespoons of the batter into the prepared tin, then scatter the batter with the plum quarters.

3 For the topping, work the flour and oats into the reserved 2 tablespoons of the batter to make a flapjack-like dough. Crumble this over the tin and scatter with the chopped ginger. Bake for 30 minutes or until golden and risen, then cool completely in the tin. Cut into squares to serve.

PER SQUARE 248 kcals, protein 4g, carbs 33g, fat 11g, sat fat 6g, fibre 2g, sugar 18g, salt 0.1g

Margaret's caramel nut squares

Margaret Fineran, who created this recipe, was a chef at the American Embassy in London.

🕐 1¼ hours, plus 4 hours freezing   🥧 9

- whipped cream, to serve

FOR THE PASTRY
- 175g/6oz plain flour, plus extra for dusting
- 50g/2oz icing sugar
- 85g/3oz cold butter, cut into cubes
- ¼ tsp vanilla extract
- 1 small egg, beaten

FOR THE FILLING
- 85g/3oz granulated sugar
- 175g/6oz clear honey
- 50g/2oz butter
- 284ml pot double cream
- 100g/4oz pecan nuts, toasted
- 100g/4oz flaked almonds, toasted
- 100g/4oz whole hazelnuts, toasted
- 100g/4oz pistachio nuts, unsalted, toasted
- 50g/2oz dried cranberries

1 Heat oven to180C/160C fan/gas 4. Whizz together the flour, icing sugar and butter for the pastry. Add the vanilla and beaten egg, and pulse until the pastry comes together. Chill, wrapped in cling film, for 30 minutes.

2 Roll the pastry out on a lightly floured surface and use to line a 23cm-square tin. Pre-bake for 7 minutes. Bring the sugar and honey for the filling to the boil without stirring. In a separate pan, heat the butter with the cream until hot. When the sugar mixture is boiling, pour in the hot cream and butter, and simmer, stirring, for 2–3 minutes.

3 Mix the nuts and cranberries into the sugary cream. Spoon the mix into the hot pastry case. Return to the oven for 7 minutes. Remove from the oven, cool, then cover and freeze for 3–4 hours. Cut into squares, thaw for 30 minutes and serve with the cream.

PER SQUARE 743 kcals, protein 10g, carbs 54g, fat 55g, sat fat 19g, fibre 3g, sugar 31g, salt 0.35g

Sunshine bars

· ·

The solution for any picnic or open-air event – packed with good things and easy to make.

🕐 25 minutes, plus 2 hours setting   🕒 18

- 100g/4oz dried ready-to-eat tropical medley or other mixed dried fruits
- 100g/4oz porridge oats
- 50g/2oz puffed rice cereal, such as Rice Krispies
- 85g/3oz desiccated coconut
- 50g/2oz blanched hazelnuts or shelled peanuts or other nuts
- 50g/2oz sunflower, sesame or pumpkin seeds
- 100g/4oz light muscovado sugar
- 125ml/4fl oz golden syrup
- 100g/4oz butter, cut into pieces

1 Chop the tropical medley into pieces using kitchen scissors. Tip the oats, cereal, coconut and dried fruit into a large bowl, and mix well. Put the hazelnuts, peanuts or other nuts and the sunflower, sesame or pumpkin seeds in a large frying pan with no oil and, over a moderate heat, stir until they are lightly toasted. Leave to cool a little then tip into the bowl and mix.

2 Put the sugar, syrup and butter in a small pan and heat gently, stirring with a wooden spoon until melted, then simmer for 2 minutes until slightly thicker and syrupy. Quickly stir the syrup into the dry ingredients, mixing until well blended with no dry patches.

3 Quickly tip the oaty mix into a 20cm-square tin and press down with the back of a spoon to even out the surface. Leave to cool and set – about 2 hours. Cut the mixture into 18 bars.

· ·

PER BAR 190 kcals, protein 2g, carbs 22g, fat 11g, sat fat 6g, fibre 2g, sugar 11g, salt 0.26g

Classic flapjacks

· ·

By using different-sized tins and varying the cooking time, this recipe can be adapted to suit all tastes.

🕐 35 minutes   🥧 12

- 175g/6oz butter, cut into pieces
- 140g/5oz golden syrup
- 50g/2oz light muscovado sugar
- 250g/9oz oats

1 Heat oven to 180C/160C fan/gas 4. Line the base of a shallow 23cm-square tin with a sheet of baking paper if the tin is not non-stick. (Use a 20cm-square tin for a thicker, chewier flapjack.) Put the butter, syrup and sugar in a medium pan. Stir over a low heat until the butter has melted and the sugar has dissolved. Remove from the heat and stir in the oats.

2 Press the mixture into the tin. Bake for 20–25 minutes, until golden brown on top (follow the longer cooking time for a crispier flapjack). Allow to cool in the tin for 5 minutes then mark into bars or squares with the back of a knife while still warm. Cool in the tin completely before cutting and removing – this prevents the flapjack from breaking up.

· ·

PER FLAPJACK 242 kcals, protein 3g, carbs 29g, fat 14g, sat fat 8g, fibre 1g, sugar 13g, salt 0.38g

Raspberry & pine-nut bars

· · · · · · · · · · · · · · · · · · · ·

This easy-mix bar is the perfect bake – all you do is weigh, mix and scatter everything into the tin.

🕐 1 hour   🥧 12

- 200g/8oz plain flour
- 200g/8oz porridge oats
- 250g pack butter, cut into small pieces and softened
- 175g/6oz light muscovado sugar
- finely grated zest 1 lemon
- 100g pack pine nuts
- 250g/9oz raspberries

1 Heat oven to 190C/170C fan/gas 5. Butter a shallow 23cm-square tin. Tip the flour, oats and butter into a mixing bowl, and work together with your fingers to make coarse crumbs. Mix in the sugar, lemon zest and three-quarters of the pine nuts using your hands, then press the mixture together well so it forms large sticky clumps.

2 Drop about two-thirds of the oat mixture into the tin, spread it out and press down very lightly – don't pack it too firmly. Scatter the raspberries on top, sprinkle the rest of the oat mixture over, then the rest of the pine nuts and press everything down lightly.

3 Bake for 35–40 minutes until pale golden on top. Cut into 12 bars with a sharp knife while still warm, then leave to cool in the tin before removing.

· ·

PER BAR 391 kcals, protein 6g, carbs 40g, fat 24g, sat fat 12g, fibre 3g, sugar 15g, salt 0.41g

Starry toffee cake squares

· ·

These cakes are truly scrumptious and so simple to whip together.

🕐 1½ hours   🥧 24

- 200g/8oz butter, plus extra for greasing
- 200g/8oz golden syrup
- 300g/10oz self-raising flour
- 1 tsp salt
- 200g/8oz light muscovado sugar
- 3 eggs
- 2 tbsp milk
- 200g/8oz yellow marzipan
- red and green food colouring
- icing sugar, for dusting

1 Heat oven to 160C/140C fan/gas 3. Butter and line the base of a 32 x 23 x 2cm Swiss roll tin. Gently melt the butter and syrup in a pan, stirring to combine. Cool for 15 minutes.

2 Sift the flour with the salt and stir in the muscovado sugar. Beat in the cooled syrup mixture. Beat the eggs and milk, and combine with the flour mixture until smooth. Pour into the tin and level with a spoon. Bake for 40–50 minutes until risen and firm in the centre. Leave in the tin to cool for 10 minutes. Tip on to a wire rack until cold.

3 Divide the marzipan into three; colour one piece with red and another with green colouring. Thickly roll out each piece and cut out star shapes. Cut the cake into 24 squares, top with marzipan stars and dust with icing sugar.

PER SQUARE 217 kcals, protein 3g, carbs 34g, fat 9g, sat fat 5g, fibre 1g, sugar 22g, salt 0.37g

Golden orange & walnut flapjacks

This is one of those great treats that you can just sling together and bake.

 55 minutes 12

- 250g/9oz unsalted butter, chopped into pieces, plus extra for greasing
- 250g/9oz golden caster sugar
- 175g/6oz golden syrup
- 425g/15oz porridge oats
- 50g/2oz walnut pieces
- finely grated zest 1 large orange
- 3 tbsp fine-cut orange marmalade

1 Heat oven to 180C/160C fan/gas 4 and generously butter a 28 x 18cm shallow baking tin. Melt the butter, sugar and syrup over a medium heat, stirring all the time. Take off the heat and stir in the oats, walnuts and orange zest. The mixture should be quite soft.

2 Tip the mixture into the tin and level it off. Bake for about 30 minutes, until the edges are golden brown but the centre is still a little soft. Remove the flapjack mixture from the oven and mark into 12 pieces while it is still warm, cutting halfway through with a knife. Leave to cool.

3 Heat the marmalade with 1 tablespoon water until it becomes syrupy. Brush this glaze over the flapjack mixture and leave to cool before cutting into 12 pieces. The flapjacks will keep in an airtight tin for up to a week.

PER FLAPJACK 455 kcals, protein 7g, carbs 60g, fat 22g, sat fat 12g, fibre 4g, sugar 36g, salt 0.12g

Bramley apple, fig & walnut flapjacks

Combining fruit with fibre is a great energy boost.

🕐 1¼ hours 🥧 9

- 450g/1lb Bramley apples, peeled and cored
- 25g/1oz golden caster sugar
- grated zest 1 small lemon
- 100g/4oz dried ready-to-eat figs, roughly chopped
- 140g/5oz butter, cut in pieces
- 50g/2oz light muscovado sugar
- 140g/5oz golden syrup
- 250g/9oz porridge oats
- ½ tsp ground cinnamon
- 25g/1oz walnuts, finely chopped

1 Heat oven to 190C/170C fan/gas 5. Slice the apples into a small pan and stir in the caster sugar. Bring to the boil, cover and simmer for 10 minutes or until the apple is soft, stirring occasionally. Stir in the zest and figs, and cook for a further 15 minutes, uncovered, stirring often until the figs are softened and the mixture is quite dry. Whizz to a purée in a food processor.

2 Melt the butter, muscovado sugar and syrup in a pan, but don't let it boil. Stir in the oats and cinnamon, and mix well.

3 Press half the mixture into a shallow 18cm square sandwich tin. Spread the purée on top and cover with the remaining mixture. Sprinkle over the walnut pieces and bake for 25 minutes or until golden. Remove from the oven, mark into squares and cool.

PER FLAPJACK 516 kcals, protein 6g, carbs 66g, fat 27g, sat fat 14g, fibre 5g, sugar 24g, salt 0.61g

Cranberry, pumpkin-seed & caramel flapjacks

· · · · · · · · · · · · · · · · · · · ·

Salted butter balances the sweetness of the caramel and dried fruits in this indulgent traybake made from rolled oats.

🕐 55 minutes   🍰 16

- 250g pack salted butter
- 6 tbsp caramel, from 397g can Carnation caramel (use remainder for the topping)
- 50g/2oz golden caster sugar
- 350g/12oz rolled oats
- 85g/3oz self-raising flour

FOR THE TOPPING

- 50g/2oz salted butter
- 25g/1oz pumpkin seeds
- 50g/2oz dried cranberries
- 25g/1oz dark chocolate chips

1 Heat oven to 160C/140C fan/gas 3 and line a 22cm-square cake tin with baking parchment. Melt the butter, 6 tablespoons of the caramel and the sugar in a large pan, then tip in the oats and flour. Stir well, making sure every oat is covered in the buttery mixture, then tip into the cake tin and press down firmly with the back of a spoon to level the surface. Bake for 40 minutes.

2 Meanwhile, make the topping. Tip the remaining caramel into a small pan with the butter and bubble for 5 minutes, stirring continuously, until the mixture turns dark golden brown and thickens a little. When the flapjacks have finished cooking, remove them from the oven and pour over the hot caramel. Leave to cool for 5 minutes, then scatter with the seeds, cranberries and chocolate chips. Leave to cool completely in the tin before cutting into squares.

· ·

PER FLAPJACK 318 kcals, protein 5g, carbs 30g, fat 19g, sat fat 11g, fibre 3g, sugar 13g, salt 0.4g

Apple & apricot treacle tart bars

This bar is deservedly a *Good Food* favourite.

🕐 1½ hours　　🥧 12

FOR THE SHORTBREAD BASE
- 100g/4oz butter, softened, plus extra for greasing
- 50g/2oz light muscovado sugar
- 175g/6oz plain flour

FOR THE FRUIT FILLING
- 450g/1lb (about 2 medium) cooking apples, cored, peeled and chopped
- 25g/1oz caster sugar
- 175g/6oz ready-to-eat dried apricots, halved

FOR THE TREACLE-TART TOPPING
- grated rind 1 orange, plus 1 tbsp juice
- 200g/8oz golden syrup
- 8 tbsp porridge oats

1 Heat oven to 160C/140C fan/gas 3. Beat the butter and sugar for the shortbread base until fluffy. Stir in the flour until smooth. Tip the mixture into a 23cm-square tin and press down on the base. Lightly prick with a fork and bake for 15 minutes. Set aside to cool.

2 Put the apples for the filling in a pan with the sugar. Cover loosely and cook over a low heat, stirring occasionally, for about 10 minutes or until the apples are pulpy. Add the apricots and cook gently, uncovered, for a further 15 minutes, stirring. Whizz to a purée.

3 Increase oven to 190C/170C fan/gas 5. Spread the filling over the base. Combine the topping ingredients until well mixed. Spread over the filling. Return to the oven for a further 20–30 minutes, until set and pale golden. Cool in the tin before cutting into bars.

PER BAR 251 kcals, protein 3g, carbs 45g, fat 8g, sat fat 5g, fibre 3g, sugar 20g, salt 0.29g

Breakfast munching muffins
. . . .

Containing marmalade, muesli, orange juice and dried apricots, these muffins make a wonderful start to your day.

🕐 1 hour, plus 20 minutes soaking   🍽 12

- 100g/4oz ready-to-eat dried apricots, chopped
- 4 tbsp orange juice
- 2 eggs
- 142ml pot soured cream
- 100ml/3½fl oz sunflower oil
- 85g/3oz golden caster sugar
- 300g/10oz self-raising flour, sifted, plus a little extra
- 1 tsp baking powder
- 50g/2oz crunchy muesli
- 12 heaped tsp marmalade

FOR THE TOPPING
- 50g/2oz light muscovado sugar
- 2 tbsp sunflower oil
- 50g/2oz crunchy muesli

1 Heat oven to 190C/170C fan/gas 5. Soak the apricots in the orange juice for 20 minutes or so to plump them up.

2 Beat the eggs in a medium bowl, then mix in the soured cream, oil and sugar. Stir into the apricot mixture. Put the flour, baking powder and muesli in a large bowl, then gently stir in the creamy apricot mixture. Combine thoroughly but quickly – don't overmix or the muffins will be tough.

3 Spoon the mixture into 12 muffin cases (the large paper cases) in a muffin tin. Dip your thumb into a little flour, then make a fairly deep thumbprint in each muffin. Fill each with 1 heaped teaspoon of the marmalade.

4 Combine the topping ingredients and sprinkle over the top of the muffins. Bake for 25–30 minutes, until well risen and golden.

. . . .
PER MUFFIN 322 kcals, protein 5g, carbs 48g, fat 14g, sat fat 3g, fibre 2g, sugar 19g, salt 0.51g

Fruity morning muffins

Make muffins healthier with mashed banana and apple sauce for natural sweetness, plus blueberries and seeds for an extra nutritious hit.

 45 minutes   12

- 2 eggs
- 150ml pot natural low-fat yogurt
- 50ml/2fl oz rapeseed oil
- 100g/4oz apple sauce or puréed apples (find with the baby food)
- 1 ripe banana, mashed
- 4 tbsp clear honey
- 1 tsp vanilla extract
- 200g/8oz wholemeal flour
- 50g/2oz rolled oats, plus extra for sprinkling
- 1½ tsp baking powder
- 1½ tsp bicarbonate of soda
- 1½ tsp ground cinnamon
- 100g/4oz blueberries
- 2 tbsp mixed seeds (we used pumpkin, sunflower and flaxseed)

1 Heat oven to 180C/160C fan/gas 4. Line a 12-hole muffin tin with 12 large muffin cases. In a jug, mix the eggs, yogurt, oil, apple sauce or purée, banana, honey and vanilla. Tip the remaining ingredients, except the seeds, into a large bowl, add a pinch of salt and mix to combine.

2 Pour the wet ingredients into the dry and mix briefly until you have a smooth batter – don't overmix as this will make the muffins heavy. Divide the batter among the cases. Sprinkle the muffins with the extra oats and the seeds. Bake for 25–30 minutes until golden and well risen, and a skewer inserted into the centre of a muffin comes out clean. Remove from the oven, transfer to a wire rack and leave to cool. Can be stored in a sealed container for up to 3 days.

PER MUFFIN 179 kcals, protein 5g, carbs 23g, fat 7g, sat fat 1g, fibre 3g, sugar 10g, salt 0.6g

Doughnut muffins

These individual sugar-dipped cupcakes are baked not fried but taste just as delicious and are best eaten straight from the oven.

🕐 40 minutes   🥧 12

- 140g/5oz butter, melted, plus extra for greasing
- 140g/5oz golden caster sugar, plus 200g/8oz extra for dusting
- 200g/8oz plain flour
- 1 tsp bicarbonate of soda
- 100ml/3½fl oz natural yogurt
- 2 eggs, beaten
- 1 tsp vanilla extract
- 12 tsp seedless raspberry jam

1 Heat oven to 190C/170C fan/gas 5. Lightly grease a 12-hole muffin tin (or use a silicone one). Put the sugar, flour and bicarb in a bowl, and mix to combine. In a jug, whisk together the yogurt, eggs and vanilla. Tip the jug contents and melted butter into the dry ingredients, and quickly fold with a metal spoon to combine.

2 Divide two-thirds of the mixture among the muffin holes. Carefully put 1 teaspoon of the jam into the centre of each, then cover with the remaining muffin mixture. Bake for 16–18 minutes until risen, golden and springy to the touch.

3 Leave the muffins to cool for 5 minutes before lifting out of the tin and rolling in the extra sugar.

PER MUFFIN 229 kcals, protein 3g, carbs 29g, fat 11g, sat fat 6g, fibre 1g, sugar 18g, salt 0.4g

Blackberry muffins

Other seasonal berries such as raspberries, loganberries and blueberries also add a delicious fruitiness to these muffins.

🕐 30 minutes   🥧 12

- 85g/3oz butter, melted, plus extra for greasing
- 400g/14oz plain flour
- 175g/6oz caster sugar
- 1 tbsp baking powder
- finely grated zest 1 orange
- ½ tsp salt
- 284ml carton buttermilk
- 2 eggs, beaten
- 250g/9oz blackberries

1 Heat oven to 200C/180C fan/gas 6. Butter a 12-hole muffin tin. In a large bowl, combine the flour, sugar, baking powder, zest and salt. In a separate bowl, mix together the buttermilk, eggs and melted butter.

2 Make a well in the centre of the dry ingredients and pour in the buttermilk mixture. Stir until the ingredients are just combined and the mixture is quite stiff, but be careful not to overmix. Lightly fold in the blackberries, then spoon the mixture into the tins to fill the holes generously.

3 Bake for 15–18 minutes until risen and pale golden on top. Leave to cool in the tin for a few minutes, as the muffins are quite delicate when hot. Run a palette knife around the edge of the muffins and carefully transfer to a wire rack to cool. Best eaten the same day.

PER MUFFIN 252 kcals, protein 5g, carbs 44g, fat 7g, sat fat 4g, fibre 2g, sugar 15g, salt 0.79g

Strawberry-cheesecake muffins

Each muffin hides a surprise filling of fresh fruit and creamy cheese.

 40 minutes 12

- 350g/12oz plain flour
- 1½ tbsp baking powder
- 140g/5oz caster sugar
- finely grated zest 2 medium oranges
- ½ tsp salt
- 2 eggs
- 250ml/9fl oz milk
- 85g/3oz butter, melted

FOR THE FILLING

- 175g/6oz half-fat soft cheese
- 3 tbsp caster sugar
- 6 small strawberries, halved

1 Heat oven to 200C/180C fan/gas 6. Line a muffin tin with 12 large paper cases. Sift the flour and baking powder into a large bowl, then stir in the sugar, orange zest and salt. Beat the eggs and milk together in a jug or bowl, then stir in the butter and gently mix into the dry ingredients to make a loose, slightly lumpy mixture. Do not overmix or the muffins will be tough.

2 Mix together the soft cheese and sugar for the filling. Half-fill the paper cases with the muffin mixture, then push half a strawberry into each. Top with a teaspoon of sweet cheese, then spoon over the remaining muffin mixture to cover and fill the muffin cases.

3 Bake for 15 minutes until well risen and golden on top. Remove from the tin and allow to cool completely on a wire rack.

PER MUFFIN 293 kcals, protein 6g, carbs 42g, fat 12g, sat fat 5g, fibre 1g, sugar 18g, salt 1.03g

Banana and Lemon Muffins

Banana chips add extra flavour and a crunchy texture to these muffins.

🕐 45 minutes   🥧 7

- 85g/3oz honey-dipped dried banana chips
- 140g/5oz self-raising flour
- 2 tsp baking powder
- finely grated zest and juice of 1 lemon
- 4 tbsp light muscovado sugar
- 5 tbsp milk
- 1 egg, beaten
- 50ml/2fl oz sunflower oil
- 3 bananas
- 4 tbsp icing sugar

1 Preheat the oven to 200°C/Gas 6/fan oven 180°C. Lightly oil seven cups of a muffin tin or line with deep paper cases. Break 50g/2oz of the banana chips into pieces. Sift together the flour and baking powder. Stir in the zest, sugar and the broken dried banana chips.

2 Whisk together the milk, egg and oil. Mash the bananas with 1 tablespoon of lemon juice. Fold carefully into the dry ingredients with the egg mixture (do not overwork it). Divide the mixture between the muffin cups/cases, not quite filling them. Bake for 20 minutes until risen and firm. Leave for a few minutes, then transfer to a wire rack to cool.

3 Sift the icing sugar into a bowl. Blend with 1–2 teaspoons of the remaining lemon juice. Drizzle over the muffins; decorate with the remaining whole banana chips.

PER MUFFIN 332 kcals, protein 4g, carbs 57g, fat 11g, sat fat 1g, fibre 1g, sugar 25g, salt 0.76g

Banana-pecan muffins

· ·

If you like the taste of banana loaf, you'll love these moist muffins.

🕐 40 minutes   🥧 8

- 85g/3oz butter, melted, plus extra for greasing
- 250g/9oz plain flour
- 25g/1oz natural wheatgerm
- 1 tsp bicarbonate of soda
- 1 tsp baking powder
- ½ tsp ground cinnamon
- 100g/4oz pecan nuts, roughly chopped
- 3 small bananas (about 350g/12oz total in their skins)
- 1 egg, beaten
- 100g/4oz light muscovado sugar
- 175ml/6fl oz buttermilk

1 Heat oven to 200C/180C fan/gas 6. Butter eight holes of a muffin tin. In a large bowl, combine the flour, wheatgerm, bicarb, baking powder, cinnamon and 85g/3oz of the pecans. Peel and mash the bananas.

2 In a separate bowl, mix together the egg, melted butter and sugar, then stir in the mashed banana and buttermilk. Add the egg mixture all at once to the flour mixture, stirring until just combined, but don't overmix or the result will be heavy.

3 Spoon the mixture into the holes to fill. Sprinkle with the remaining pecans. Bake for 20–25 minutes until well risen and golden. Leave in the tin for 10 minutes, then remove and cool on a wire rack.

· ·

PER MUFFIN 376 kcals, protein 7g, carbs 47g, fat 19g, sat fat 6g, fibre 2g, sugar 13g, salt 0.89g·

Squash, cinnamon & pumpkin seed muffins

· · · · · · · · · · · · · · · · · · · ·

This mixture will also divide between a 12-hole muffin tin for smaller muffins.

🕐 50 minutes · 🥧 9

- 280g/10oz plain flour
- 1 tbsp baking powder
- 2 tsp ground cinnamon
- 1 tsp salt
- 3 eggs
- 175ml/6fl oz milk
- 85g/3oz butter, melted
- 175g/6oz light muscovado sugar
- 350g/12oz peeled, grated butternut squash
- small handful of green pumpkin seeds

1 Preheat the oven to 200°C/Gas 6/fan oven 180°C. Lightly butter a 9-hole muffin tin or line with paper muffin cases. Sift together the flour, baking powder, cinnamon and salt and put aside.

2 In a large bowl, mix the eggs, milk and butter. Add the sugar and beat well. Add the flour mixture and beat to give a lumpy batter. Stir in the grated squash.

3 Fill the nine holes of the muffin tin (or paper cases) to the top with the mixture, sprinkle the pumpkin seeds on top. Bake for 20–25 minutes until well risen and firm to the touch. Cool slightly in the tin, turn out and cool on a wire rack.

· ·

PER MUFFIN 317 kcals, protein 7g, carbs 50g, fat 12g, sat fat 6g, fibre 2g, sugar 20g, salt 1.52g

Feel-good muffins

These muffins have the bonus of lots of health-giving ingredients – so enjoy them without guilt!

 45 minutes   6-8

- butter, for greasing
- 175g/6oz self-raising flour
- 50g/2oz porridge oats
- 140g/5oz light muscovado sugar
- 2 tsp ground cinnamon
- ½ tsp bicarbonate of soda
- 1 egg, beaten
- 150ml/¼ pint buttermilk
- 1 tsp vanilla extract
- 6 tbsp sunflower oil
- 175g/6oz stoned prunes, chopped
- 85g/3oz pecan nuts

1 Heat oven to 200C/180C fan/gas 6. Butter six or eight muffin tins or line them with muffin cases. Put the flour, oats, sugar, cinnamon and bicarbonate of soda in a large bowl, then rub everything through your fingers, as if making pastry, to ensure the ingredients are evenly blended.

2 In a separate bowl, beat the egg, then stir in the buttermilk, vanilla and oil. Lightly stir the egg mixture into the flour crumb. Fold in the prunes and nuts.

3 Divide among the tins, filling the cases to the brim, then bake for 20–25 minutes until risen and golden. Serve warm or cold.

PER MUFFIN (6) 478 kcals, protein 8g, carbs 66g, fat 22g, sat fat 2g, fibre 2g, sugar 24g, salt 0.66g

Berry buttermilk muffins

Although best made with fresh blueberries, you can make these muffins using the same amount of frozen berries.

🕐 40 minutes　🥧 12

- 85g/3oz butter, melted, plus extra for greasing
- 400g/14oz plain flour
- 175g/6oz caster sugar
- 1 tbsp baking powder
- finely grated zest 1 lemon
- ½ tsp salt
- 284ml carton buttermilk
- 2 eggs, beaten
- 250g/9oz fresh or frozen blueberries, or mixed summer fruits, used straight from frozen

1 Heat oven to 200C/180C fan/gas 6. Butter a 12-hole muffin tin. In a large bowl, combine the flour, sugar, baking powder, lemon zest and salt. In a separate bowl, mix together the buttermilk, eggs and melted butter.

2 Make a well in the centre of the dry ingredients and pour in the buttermilk mixture. Stir until the ingredients are just combined and the mixture is quite stiff, but don't overmix. Lightly fold in the berries, then spoon the mixture into the tins to fill generously.

3 Bake for about 25 minutes until risen and pale golden on top. Leave to cool in the tin for about 5 minutes before turning out carefully on to a wire rack, as the muffins are quite delicate when hot.

PER MUFFIN 253 kcals, protein 5g, carbs 44g, fat 7g, sat fat 4g, fibre 1g, sugar 15g, salt 0.91g

Marmalade muffins

· ·

These muffins are filled with oats and citrus flavours and have a melting middle.
They are delicious and low-fat too.

🕐 25 minutes   🥧 9

- 175g/6oz plain flour
- 25g/1oz porridge oats, plus extra for sprinkling
- 175g/6oz light soft brown sugar
- 1 tsp baking powder
- ½ tsp bicarbonate of soda
- zest and juice 1 orange
- 1 tbsp sunflower oil
- 150g pot natural yogurt
- 1 egg
- 9 tsp chunky marmalade

1 Heat oven to 200C/180C fan/gas 6 and line a muffin tin with nine paper cases. Combine the flour, oats, sugar, baking powder and bicarb in a bowl. Whisk the orange zest and juice, oil, yogurt and egg together in a jug with a fork, then lightly stir the two mixtures together until just combined.

2 Spoon 1 tablespoon of the mixture into each muffin case, top with 1 teaspoon of the marmalade, then cover with the remaining muffin mix and a sprinkling of oats. Bake for 15–20 minutes until cooked through and golden, then leave to cool slightly.

· ·

PER MUFFIN 206 kcals, protein 4g, carbs 41g, fat 3g, sat fat 1g, fibre 1g, sugar 26g, salt 0.4g

Cranberry & poppy seed muffins

Serve these muffins warm, drizzled with a generous helping of maple syrup.

🕐 50 minutes   🥧 10

- oil, for greasing
- 100g/4oz unsalted butter
- 284ml carton soured cream
- 2 eggs
- 1 tsp vanilla extract
- 300g/10oz plain flour
- 2 tsp baking powder
- 1 tsp bicarbonate of soda
- ½ tsp salt
- 200g/8oz golden caster sugar
- 4 tsp poppy seeds
- 140g/5oz fresh or frozen cranberries (thawed)
- maple syrup, to serve

1 Heat oven to 190C/170C fan/gas 5. Line ten holes of a muffin tin with large discs of very loosely scrunched and lightly oiled greaseproof paper (they should come up the sides of the tin holes so they become paper muffin cases). Melt the butter in a large pan, leave to cool for a minute or two, then beat in the soured cream, followed by the eggs and the vanilla extract.

2 Mix the flour, baking powder, bicarbonate of soda, salt, sugar and poppy seeds together in a bowl. Stir this into the soured-cream mixture along with the cranberries.

3 Fill each of the prepared muffin cases generously with the mixture and bake for 20–25 minutes. Test with a skewer – it should pull out clean if muffins are done. Lift on to a cooling rack, spoon over some maple syrup and eat while they are still warm.

PER MUFFIN 340 kcals, protein 6g, carbs 45g, fat 16g, sat fat 9g, fibre 1g, sugar 21g, salt 0.98g

Triple-chocolate-chunk muffins

No chance of keeping these for more than a day – definitely a muffin to eat while still warm and the chocolate is gooey.

🕐 35 minutes 🥧 11

- 85g/3oz butter, melted, plus extra for greasing
- 250g/9oz plain flour
- 25g/1oz cocoa powder
- 2 tsp baking powder
- ½ tsp bicarbonate of soda
- 85g/3oz each dark and white chocolate, broken into chunks
- 100g/4oz milk chocolate, broken into chunks
- 2 eggs, beaten
- 284ml pot soured cream
- 85g/3oz light muscovado sugar

1 Heat oven to 200C/180C fan/gas 6. Butter eleven holes of a muffin tin. In a large bowl, combine the flour, cocoa, baking powder, bicarbonate of soda and chocolate. In a separate bowl, mix together the eggs, soured cream, sugar and melted butter.

2 Add the soured-cream mixture to the flour mixture and stir until just combined and the mixture is fairly stiff, but don't overmix. Spoon the mixture into the holes to fill generously.

3 Bake for 20 minutes until well risen. Leave in the tins for about 15 minutes as the mixture is quite tender. Remove from the tins and cool on a wire rack.

PER MUFFIN 325 kcals, protein 6g, carbs 37g, fat 18g, sat fat 11g, fibre 1g, sugar 17g, salt 0.72g

Angela's all-American chocolate chunk cookies

· ·

There are no clever techniques involved with food writer Angela Nilsen's irresistible cookies – just measure, mix, stir and bake.

🕐 50 minutes   🥧 12

- 300g/10oz dark chocolate (about 55% cocoa solids), broken into small chunks
- 100g/4oz light muscovado sugar
- 85g/3oz butter, softened
- 100g/4oz crunchy peanut butter
- 1 medium egg
- ½ tsp vanilla extract
- 100g/4oz self-raising flour
- 100g bar milk chocolate, broken into small chunks
- 100g/4oz large salted roasted peanuts

1 Heat oven to 180C/160C fan/gas 4. Melt 100g/4oz of the dark-chocolate chunks in a large bowl over a pan of simmering water. Stir, then, off the heat, tip in the sugar, butter, peanut butter, egg and vanilla, and beat with a wooden spoon until well mixed. Stir in the flour, all the milk-chocolate chunks, the nuts and half the remaining dark-chocolate chunks. The mixture will feel quite soft.

2 Drop big spoonfuls in 12 piles on to two or three baking sheets, leaving room for them to spread. Stick two or three pieces of the remaining dark-chocolate chunks into each cookie.

3 Bake for 10–12 minutes until they are tinged very slightly darker around the edges. They will be soft in the middle, but will crisp up as they cool. Cook for longer and you'll have crisper cookies. Leave to cool for a few minutes, then transfer to a wire rack.

· ·

PER COOKIE 381 kcals, protein 7g, carbs 36g, fat 24g, sat fat 10g, fibre 2g, sugar 27g, salt 0.42g

Coconut & cashew cookies

Creamed coconut adds richness and flavour to these American-style cookies.

 35 minutes   14–16

- 140g/5oz unsalted cashew nuts, toasted
- 85g/3oz creamed coconut, grated
- 175g/6oz plain flour
- ½ tsp baking powder
- 140g/5oz butter, softened, plus extra for greasing
- 125g/4½oz dark muscovado sugar
- 1 tbsp ground ginger
- 1 egg

1 Heat oven to 180C/160C fan/gas 4. Split some cashews in half; leave the rest whole. Mix with the coconut in a small bowl.

2 Blend the remaining ingredients in a food processor to make a smooth, stiff consistency. Set aside 4 tablespoonfuls of the nut mixture; stir the rest into the flour mixture.

3 Put 14–16 heaped tablespoons of the mixture in mounds, well apart, on buttered baking sheets. Flatten slightly with your fingers. Sprinkle with the reserved nut mixture and bake for 10–12 minutes until golden and set at the edges. Leave for a few minutes, then cool on a wire rack. The cookies will stay fresh for up to 1 week in an airtight container.

PER COOKIE (14) 262 kcals, protein 4g, carbs 22g, fat 18g, sat fat 9g, fibre 2g, sugar 9g, salt 0.34g

Smarties cookies

Make these treats for your next birthday party – for kids or adults.

 20 minutes 14

- 100g/4oz butter, softened
- 100g/4oz light muscovado sugar
- 1 tbsp golden syrup
- 150g/5½oz self-raising flour
- 85g/3oz Smarties (about 3 tubes)

1 Heat oven to 180C/160C fan/gas 4. Beat the butter and sugar in a bowl until light and creamy, then beat in the syrup.
2 Work in half the flour. Stir in the Smarties with the remaining flour and work the dough together with your fingers. Divide into 14 balls. Put the balls well apart on baking sheets. Do not flatten them.
3 Bake for 12 minutes until pale golden at the edges. Cool on a wire rack. These cookies will keep for up to 4 days in an airtight tin.

PER COOKIE 167 kcals, protein 2g, carbs 23g, fat 8g, sat fat 5g, fibre trace, sugar 13g, salt 0.3g

Oaty cherry cookies

· ·

Store any uncooked mixture in the fridge for up to 1 week, or freeze on the day for up to 6 months, defrosting before baking.

🕐 30 minutes   🥧 18

- 250g/9oz butter, softened
- 50g/2oz caster sugar
- 100g/4oz light muscovado sugar
- 150g/5½oz self-raising flour
- 200g/8oz porridge oats
- 200g/8oz glacé cherries
- 50g/2oz raisins

1 Heat oven to 180C/160C fan/gas 4. Line two or three baking sheets with non-stick baking paper (or bake in batches). In a bowl, beat the butter and sugars together until light and fluffy. Stir in the flour and oats, and mix well. Roughly chop three-quarters of the cherries, then stir these and the remaining whole cherries and the raisins into the oat mixture.

2 Divide the mixture into 18 equal portions. Roughly shape each portion into a ball. Put on the baking sheets well apart to allow for spreading. Lightly flatten each biscuit with your fingertips, keeping the mixture quite rough-looking.

3 Bake for 15–20 minutes until the cookies are pale golden around the edges, but still feel soft in the centre. Cool on the baking sheets for 5 minutes, then transfer to a wire rack to finish cooling.

· ·

PER COOKIE 249 kcals, protein 2g, carbs 33g, fat 13g, sat fat 7g, fibre 1g, sugar 15g, salt 0.36g

Lemon & sultana cookies

Swap the sultanas for chopped nuts or other dried fruit to vary the recipe for these American-style cookies.

🕐 30 minutes   🥧 30

- 140g/5oz butter, cut into small pieces, plus extra for greasing
- 350g/12oz plain flour
- ½ tsp baking powder
- ½ tsp bicarbonate of soda
- 175g/6oz caster sugar
- 85g/3oz sultanas
- 100g/4oz lemon curd
- 2 eggs, beaten

FOR THE ICING
- 100g/4oz sifted icing sugar
- 2 tbsp lemon juice

1 Heat oven to 200C/180C fan/gas 6. Butter three baking sheets (or bake in several batches). Sift the flour, baking powder and bicarbonate of soda into a bowl. Add the butter and rub in with your fingertips until the mixture resembles fine breadcrumbs.

2 Stir in the sugar and sultanas, add the lemon curd and eggs, and mix to a soft dough. Shape the dough into 30 small balls, about 2.5cm/1in wide, and put on the baking sheets, allowing plenty of space between them so they can spread. Using your fingers, gently press the top of each biscuit to flatten it slightly.

3 Bake for 12–15 minutes until risen and light golden. Leave to cool for 1 minute on the baking sheets, then transfer to a wire rack to cool completely. Blend the icing sugar and lemon juice, then drizzle over each cookie.

PER COOKIE 134 kcals, protein 2g, carbs 23g, fat 5g, sat fat 3g, fibre trace, sugar 11g, salt 0.2g

Pine-nut cookies

· ·

Traditionally made with vegetable shortening, this old-fashioned type of cookie dough can also be made into a case for a fruit tart.

🕐 1 hour 📋 18

- 50g/2oz pine nuts, plus a few extra to decorate
- 175g/6oz butter, softened, plus extra for greasing
- 140g/5oz golden granulated sugar, plus extra for sprinkling
- seeds from 1 star anise, crushed (optional)
- 1 egg
- 250g/9oz plain flour
- 1 tsp baking powder

1 Toast the pine nuts in a dry heavy-based pan for 1–2 minutes. Set aside.

2 Put the butter, sugar and star anise seeds, if using, in a food processor, and whizz for 1 minute. Scrape down the bowl, then whizz again briefly. Add the egg and whizz again. Tip in the flour and baking powder, and whizz until the mixture forms a dough. Mix in the pine nuts (reserving enough for step 3), then chill for 30 minutes, wrapped in plastic film.

3 Heat oven to 180C/160C fan/gas 4. Divide the chilled dough into 18 walnut-sized pieces and press out into 5cm/2in rounds, level but not too neat. Put on the baking sheets and press 2 pine nuts on the top of each. Bake for 15 minutes until pale golden. Transfer to a wire rack to cool, sprinkle with sugar and serve.

· ·
PER COOKIE 176 kcals, protein 2g, carbs 20g, fat 10g, sat fat 5g, fibre trace, sugar 9g, salt 0.28g

Walnut oat biscuits

Serve with ripe Taleggio or another soft cheese, such as dolcelatte or St Andre, and a brimming bowl of fresh, juicy strawberries.

🕐 25 minutes   🍕 15

- 100g/4oz butter, softened, plus extra for greasing
- 85g/3oz light muscovado sugar
- 1 egg, beaten
- 50g/2oz porridge oats
- 50g/2oz walnuts, finely chopped
- 85g/3oz plain flour
- ½ tsp baking powder
- soft cheese and strawberries, to serve

1 Heat oven to 180C/160C fan/gas 4. Butter two baking sheets. In a bowl, beat the butter and sugar for 5 minutes by hand or 2 minutes in the food processor until light and fluffy. Beat in the egg, then stir in the oats, nuts, flour and baking powder.

2 Drop 15 dessertspoonfuls of the mixture, with a little space between to allow for spreading, on the baking sheets. Bake for 15 minutes until pale golden, then cool on a wire rack.

3 Serve the biscuits with soft cheese and strawberries. The biscuits will keep fresh in a sealed container for up to a week.

PER BISCUIT 133 kcals, protein 2g, carbs 13g, fat 9g, sat fat 4g, fibre 1g, sugar 6g, salt 0.15g

Chunky choc-orange cookies

Chocolate and orange make an irresistible combination. Best eaten while still warm from the oven for a gorgeously gooey chocolate centre.

🕐 30 minutes   🥧 18

- 250g/9oz butter, softened
- 50g/2oz caster sugar
- 100g/4oz light muscovado sugar
- 300g/10oz self-raising flour
- 2 tbsp milk
- 175g/6oz orange-flavoured dark chocolate, very roughly chopped
- 50g/2oz pecan nuts, very roughly chopped

1 Heat oven to 180C/160C fan/gas 4. Line two or three baking sheets with non-stick baking paper (or bake in batches). In a bowl, beat together the butter and sugars until light and fluffy. Stir in the flour and milk, mix well, then stir in the chocolate and nuts.
2 Divide the mixture into 18 equal portions. Roughly shape each portion into a ball. Put on the baking sheets well apart to allow for spreading. Lightly flatten each biscuit with your fingertips, keeping the mixture quite rough-looking.
3 Bake for 15–20 minutes until the cookies are pale golden around the edges, but still feel soft in the centre. Cool on the baking sheets for 5 minutes, then transfer to a wire rack and allow to cool a little more before eating.

PER COOKIE 261 kcals, protein 2g, carbs 28g, fat 16g, sat fat 9g, fibre 1g, sugar 14g, salt 0.42g

Festive almond biscuits

Light biscuits with a surprise almond filling and orange-scented sugar.

 1¼ hours   20

- 85g/3oz unsalted butter, chilled and cut into pieces, plus extra for greasing
- 110g/4oz self-raising flour
- 85g/3oz ground almonds
- 100g/4oz caster sugar
- 50g/2oz marzipan, cut into 20 cubes

FOR THE ORANGE SUGAR
- pared rind 2 oranges
- 50g/2oz icing sugar

1 Whizz the butter with the flour and almonds to a breadcrumb consistency. Add half the caster sugar; whizz until the mixture starts to cling together, then work lightly into a ball.
2 Thinly roll out half of the dough. Use 6cm/2¼in cutters to cut out 20 crescents and stars, then put them on a buttered baking sheet. Roll the marzipan cubes into sausage- or ball- shaped pieces and lay on the crecents and stars. Top each with a matching dough shape cut from the remaining dough and seal the edges. Chill for 30 minutes.
3 Heat oven to 160C/140C fan/gas 3. For the orange sugar: put the orange rind on a baking sheet and bake for 3 minutes; cool. Mix the remaining caster sugar and the icing sugar; toss with the rind. Bake the biscuits for 18–20 minutes; cool on a wire rack. Sprinkle with the orange sugar.

PER BISCUIT 109 kcals, protein 1g, carbs 14g, fat 6g, sat fat 2g, fibre 1g, sugar 9g, salt 0.06g

Anzac biscuits

· ·

These delicious biscuits were made to send to the ANZACs (Australian and New Zealand Army Corps) serving in Gallipoli.

🕐 35 minutes   🥟 20

- 85g/3oz porridge oats
- 85g/3oz desiccated coconut
- 100g/4oz plain flour
- 100g/4oz caster sugar
- 100g/4oz butter, plus extra for greasing
- 1 tbsp golden syrup
- 1 tsp bicarbonate of soda

1 Heat oven to 180C/160C fan/gas 4. Put the oats, coconut, flour and sugar in a bowl. Melt the butter in a small pan or microwave and stir in the golden syrup. Add the bicarbonate of soda to 2 tablespoons boiling water, then stir into the golden syrup-and-butter mixture.

2 Make a well in the middle of the dry ingredients and pour in the butter-and-golden syrup mixture. Stir gently to incorporate the dry ingredients.

3 Put dessertspoonfuls of the mixture on to buttered baking sheets, about 2.5cm/1in apart to allow room for spreading. Bake in batches for 8–10 minutes until golden. Transfer to a wire rack to cool.

· ·

PER BISCUIT 118 kcals, protein 1g, carbs 13g, fat 7g, sat fat 5g, fibre 1g, sugar 6g, salt 0.28g

Index

Also available from BBC Books and Good Food